COLOR MAGICK

A Colorful Array of Magickal Practices

Infuse your magickal and divination practices with the radiant energy of color. This sourcebook for color magick contains rituals, meditations, healings, and magickal correspondences.

Discover the magickal powers of the colors you wear and the subtle effects of color on your emotions. Find out how to use color in psychic development techniques, chakra balancing, divination, and all manner of spells. With the instructions in this book, you can even learn how to add color to both magickal and everyday practices, including numerology, astrology, and music.

About the Author

Raymond Buckland's first major book, *A Pocket Guide to the Supernatural* (Ace Books, New York), was published in 1969. Since then he has had thirty books published, with more than one million copies in print. His books have been translated into eleven foreign languages on subjects covering Wicca, various forms of magick, divination, folklore, and spiritualism. He has also produced novels, a video, and Gypsy fortunetelling decks. Ray lives on a small farm in Ohio.

To Write to the Author

If you wish to contact the author or would like more information about this book, please write to the author in care of Llewellyn Worldwide and we will forward your request. The author and publisher appreciate hearing from you and learning of your enjoyment of this book and how it has helped you. Llewellyn Worldwide cannot guarantee that every letter written to the author can be answered, but all will be forwarded. Please write to:

Raymond Buckland
℅ Llewellyn Worldwide
P.O. Box 64383, Dept. 0-7387-0204-8
St. Paul, MN 55164-0383, U.S.A.
Please enclose a self-addressed stamped envelope for reply,
or $1.00 to cover costs. If outside U.S.A., enclose
international postal reply coupon.

Many of Llewellyn's authors have websites with additional information and resources. For more information, please visit our website at: www.llewellyn.com

COLOR MAGICK

UNLEASH YOUR INNER POWERS

Raymond Buckland

2002
Llewellyn Publications
St. Paul, Minnesota 55164-0383, U.S.A.

FIRST EDITION, REVISED
Second Printing, 2002

Previously titled *Practical Color Magick*, first edition, thirteen printings

Book design and editing by Kimberly Nightingale
Cover design by Lisa Novak
Interior illustrations by Kevin R. Brown

Library of Congress Cataloging-in-Publication Data
Buckland, Raymond.
    Color magick: unleash your inner powers / Raymond Buckland.
      p. cm.
    Rev. ed. of: Practical color magick. 1st ed. 1983.
    Includes bibliographical references and index.
    ISBN 0-7387-0204-8
    1. Magic. 2. Occultism. 3. Parapsychology. 4. Meditation.
5. Color—Miscellanea. I. Buckland, Raymond. Practical color magick.
II. Title.

BF1623.C6 B83 2002
133.4'3—dc21   2001050563

Llewellyn Publications
A Division of Llewellyn Worldwide, Ltd.
P.O. Box 64383, Dept. 0-7387-0204-8
St. Paul, MN 55164-0383, U.S.A.
www.llewellyn.com

Printed in the United States of America

Other Books by Raymond Buckland

Advanced Candle Magic (Llewellyn, 1996)

Amazing Secrets of the Psychic World (Parker, 1975) *with Hereward Carrington*

Anatomy of the Occult (Weiser, 1977)

The Book of African Divination (Inner Traditions, 1992) *with Kathleen Binger*

Buckland's Complete Book of Witchcraft (Llewellyn, 1975, 1977, 1987)

Buckland Gypsies' Domino Divination Deck (Llewellyn, 1995)

Cardinal's Sin (Llewellyn, 1996)

Coin Divination (Llewellyn, 1999)

The Committee (Llewellyn, 1993)

Doors to Other Worlds (Llewellyn, 1993)

Gypsy Dream Dictionary (Llewellyn, 1990, 1998)

Gypsy Witchcraft & Magic (Llewellyn, 1998)

Here is the Occult (HC, 1974)

The Magic of Chant-O-Matics (Parker, 1978)

Mu Revealed (Warner Paperback Library, 1970)

Mu Revealed (Warner Paperback Library, 1970)
under the pseudonym "Tony Earll"

A Pocket Guide to the Supernatural (Ace, 1969)

Practical Candleburning Rituals (Llewellyn, 1970, 1976, 1982)

Ray Buckland's Magic Cauldron (Galde Press, 1995)

Scottish Witchcraft (Llewellyn, 1991)

Secrets of Gypsy Fortunetelling (Llewellyn, 1988)

Secrets of Gypsy Love Magic (Llewellyn, 1990)

The Tree: Complete Book of Saxon Witchcraft (Weiser, 1974)

Truth About Spirit Communication (Llewellyn, 1995)

Wicca for Life (Citadel, 2001)

The Witch Book: the Encyclopedia of Witchcraft, Wicca & Neopaganism (Visible Ink Press, 2002)

Witchcraft Ancient and Modern (HC, 1970)

Witchcraft from the Inside (Llewellyn, 1971, 1975, 1995)

Witchcraft . . . the Religion (Buckland Museum, 1966)

Tarot Kits

The Buckland Romani Tarot (2001)

Gypsy Fortunetelling Tarot Kit (1989, 1998)

Videos

Witchcraft . . . Yesterday and Today (1990)

For Tara
who brought color and magick into my life

Contents

Illustrations

Introduction

*I*n the pink . . . feeling blue . . . green with envy . . . red with anger . . . purple passion . . . rose-colored spectacles . . . a jaundiced view . . . the list goes on, showing color is very much a part of our lives. If we look closer at those opening phrases, we realize that color is also a part of our health. Since the beginning of time, colors have been endowed with magick. The ancient Egyptians used color in their temples of healing. The Chinese and the Chaldeans used it, as did the mystics of India, who associated colors with the chakras. Pythagoras used it for healing. You cannot live without color; it is your omnipresent companion throughout life. But what is color? How can it be used?

Until the seventeenth century, it was believed color was created directly through refraction of sunlight. Sir Isaac Newton was the first man, in 1666, to break down sunlight into its component colors, as it were, using a prism and producing a spectrum. The prism diffracted the white light and divided it into seven bands of color: red, orange, yellow, green, blue, indigo, and violet. In actual fact, there is an enormous, if not infinite, number of perfectly distinct colors in light. These seven colors, however, are often referred to as the primary colors; other tints and shades being produced by mixing them. In the strictest sense, there

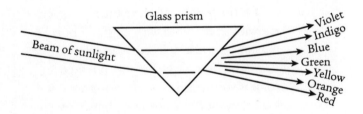

Figure 1
Newton's Experiment of 1666

are really only three primary colors: red, green, and blue-violet. These three colors cannot be resolved into any others.* These three colors, or kinds of light, when mixed together, produce white. Further, the combination of any two gives the complementary color to the third, e.g., red and light green produce yellow, which is complementary to the blue-violet.

Light travels at 186,000 miles per second. As it travels, it vibrates. Light is, in fact, radiant energy traveling in the form of waves. The rate of vibration can be measured in units known as Angstrom units (Å), measuring one ten-millionth of a millimeter. For example, the color red has a wavelength varying from 6,200Å to 6,700Å, orange from 5,900Å to 6,200Å; yellow, 5,600Å to 5,900Å; green, 5,100Å to 5,600Å; blue, 4,700Å to 5,100Å; indigo, 4,500Å to 4,700Å; and violet, 4,000Å to 4,500Å.

Our bodies select, from the sunlight, whatever colors are needed for balance, the vibrations being absorbed into us. Animals and plants do the same. Our bodies themselves, of course, vibrate, for all things radiate energy. A chair, a table, a house, a flower, a bird; everything is vibration. This can be seen in the aura and can be photographed through the Kirlian technique.

Science is still researching the exact way in which light penetrates the body. One school of thought holds that light is admitted through the eyes and thereby

---

*They should not be confused with the three primary *pigments* familiar in painting and printing: red, yellow, and blue.

stimulates the pituitary gland, causing it to secrete certain hormones. It is a proven fact, however, that there is reaction from the body to light even without vision. It is possible the skin *senses* radiation through certain cells. My own feeling—which seems to be endorsed by the science of radionics—is that when color rays strike the skin they produce complementary vibrations within the body that signal the brain and, whether by secretion of hormones from glands with resultant distribution in the blood or, however, cause reaction of the body.

The principle of healing with color (chromotherapy or chromopathy) is to give the ailing body an extra dose of any color(s) lacking. The application can be done in a variety of ways, as we shall see. Basically, the red end of the spectrum stimulates, while the blue end calms.

There are any number of experiments being conducted today, around the world, involving the use of color in such circumstances as work environment, living environment, education, and nursing. For example, the use of red, or even orange, in mental hospitals is asking for trouble. Blue has a cooling, soothing effect. Already, the stark white clothing of surgeons and their operating-room assistants has given way to pastel shades of blue and green (also soothing).

The study of color for both therapeutic and magickal use, I term *chromology* (from the Greek *kroma*, color; *logos,* discourse). The actual use of color for therapy I term *chromopathy* (Gr. *kroma,* color; *pathos,* suffering). One of the joys of color, whether used for therapy work or magick, is its practicability. It is a tool that anyone can use, inexpensively, with little instruction and, perhaps more importantly, with no danger. As with candle burning†there are no entities invoked in basic color magick. It is the use of a natural element in a practical way.

Color can be enormously helpful not only therapeutically and in the working of magick, but also in such areas as meditation, crystal- and mirror-gazing, tarot reading, absent healing, clairvoyance—in a myriad of ways embracing the full "spectrum" of the occult. We will explore some of these in the pages that follow.

---

†Read *Practical Candleburning Rituals* by Raymond Buckland, Llewellyn Publications, St. Paul, Minn., 1976.

1

Color in Meditation

These days, when talk turns to meditation, there is always mention of TM or transcendental meditation. TM's results have been excellent, though other forms of meditation have been equally so. But more and more, recently, I have been told by people in all forms of meditation, "I don't seem to be getting anything out of my meditation anymore."

This is a comment from those who have been meditating for years and also by those who have given up. Well, now the magick can be put back into meditation.

You can get something out of meditation again; for now we can go a step further with CM. CM is color meditation, or color magick; and it transcends even TM, as many people have discovered.

Meditation opens the door to individual growth and spiritual advancement. It is probably the most effective method of advancement in all fields of psychic and spiritual development and, at the same time, the most simple. It can be done in a group or it can be done alone.

What exactly is meditation? The short answer is: it is listening—listening to your inner self, to your higher being, to the collective unconscious, to the creative force, to the gods themselves. It can be all these things. And, through these things, it can bring you joy and peace, strength and understanding, life and enlightenment. It is a very ancient art, found throughout history and probably even pre-history. It is a quieting of the mind from the hub-bub of everyday living, enabling you to get away, to separate yourself from your problems, your worries, hopes, and fears. It can be a longed-for passive island in the midst of a sea of frenzied activity. That is not to say that meditation is not constructive. It is. In fact, it is far more constructive than passive.

The late, great psychic Edgar Cayce, in one of his readings (No. 281–13) said:

Meditation is emptying self of all that hinders from the creative forces rising along the natural channels of the physical man to be disseminated through those centers and sources that create the activities of the physical, the mental, the spiritual man; properly done (meditation) must make one stronger mentally, physically . . . and as we give out, so does the whole of man physically and mentally become depleted, yet entering into the silence, in meditation, with a clean hand, a clean body, a clean mind; we may receive that strength and power that fits each individual, each soul, for a greater activity in this material world.

Meditation and Kundalini

Meditation, in its present general form, has come to us from the East. Certainly, meditation has been practiced in the West for centuries but not to the extent found in the East. In tantric yoga, for example, meditation plays an essential part in the preparation for such an ancient rite as *maithuna*. Today's almost universal acceptance and use of meditation has certainly been inspired more by Eastern teachings than by any other. Through meditation, your psychic force can be sent throughout your body to the vital centers known in yoga as the chakras. This mysterious, very potent force, which dwells within all of us, is called the *kundalini* power.

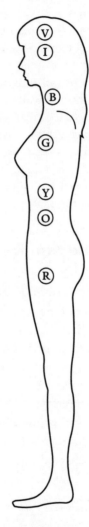

Figure 2
Colors Corresponding to Chakras

Here is how it works. The spine consists of thirty-three vertebrae forming a long, hollow column housing and protecting the spinal cord. The cord itself extends from the fourth ventricle of the brain down to the coccygeal region. Through the center of the cord passes a fine conduit known as the *canalis centralis*. It is up through this central canal that the kundalini power travels when awakened. As it travels, it touches and vitalizes your special psychic centers, the chakras.

There are seven principle chakras. They are essentially of the etheric, yet, they do coincide with various glands in the physical body: the base of the spine at the perineum, midway between the anus and the genitals; the fifth lumbar at the suprenal glands; the solar plexus at the lyden; the heart at the thymus; the throat at the thyroid; the crown of the head at the pituitary; and, the position of the third eye at the pineal (fig. 2).

These seven centers each have their own governing color. For the perineum, the color is red; for the suprarenal, orange; lyden, yellow; thymus, green; thyroid, blue; pineal, indigo, and pituitary, violet.

The seven centers correspond, as you see, to the seven colors of the light spectrum. During meditation these seven essential centers are opened as the kundalini rises. The use of colored light, in combination with the meditation, enhances this opening of the centers, reinforcing them and expanding and developing them beyond their previous limits.

It is through setting up the necessary vibrations that the sleeping serpent (kundalini) is aroused. These vibrations, then, play an important part in every one of us. To again quote Cayce (Reading No. 900–422): "All force is vibration, as all comes from one central vibration. . . . Then we see the evolution of force in vibration brought up to the point wherein man becomes one with the Creative Energy, or the Godhead."

This vibratory energy, and its relationship to color, has been measured. For example, it has been found that muscular tension, from the impacts on the retina of the eye, increases under a green light from a normal 23 empirical units to 29 units. Under a yellow light, the tension increases to 30 units. Under orange light, to 35 units and under red light, muscular tension increases from that normal 23 to as much as 42 units. We can see, then, not only that color can affect you, but that the long-wave region of the (visible) spectrum—*the red end*—also stimulates. The calorific rays of red, in fact, can raise your temperature, increase your circulation, and quicken your heartbeat. The short-wave region—the *blue end*—has the reverse influence. This is the basis for the use of color in healing.

How to Meditate

Most people meditate in a wide variety of places, wearing ordinary, everyday clothing. This is fine and can certainly be useful. If the only time you can meditate is when traveling to work on the subway, do it. But to get more out of meditation, you must put more into it. First of all, meditate at the same time every day. Whether it be morning, afternoon, or evening is up to you. There are different types of people: some of us are *night people,* others of us are *day people.* Meditate at the time of day that feels best to you. If in doubt, here is a guide: find out (if you do not already know) what time of day, or night, you were born. Meditate at the time most conveniently close to your birth time as you can. You may find this is the right time for you.

Meditate where you will not be disturbed and where it is as quiet as possible—the back of the house, away from traffic noise, perhaps. The actual physical position you adopt for meditation can again be to suit yourself. You may sit in the yoga position, you may prefer to sit on your heels, or sit in a chair, or lie flat on your back. The important thing, however, is to have your spine straight. I personally recommend that you sit in a comfortable straight-backed chair, one in which you can sit well back with your spine straight yet still have your feet flat on the floor. The chair should preferably have arms to it, on which you can rest your arms. It need not have a high back, in fact, it is better if it does not.

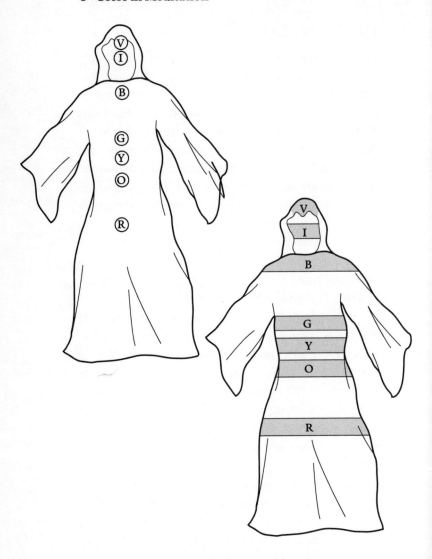

Figures 3a and 3b
Color Meditation Robe

The CM Robe

It is recommended that loose clothing be worn during meditation; particularly recommended is a CM robe.

We have discussed the association of colors with the chakras and the desirability of stimulating those colors/chakras. This can be accomplished beautifully by the simple wearing of a robe designed specifically for color meditation. Any refinement of shape can be made to suit your individual whims, but remember to not make it tight fitting. The material should be pure white. In addition to the robe itself, you need a head covering, also white and loose fitting. This hat should have a front (point) that comes down to cover the space between the eyes, where the third eye is located.

Up the front of the robe cut out large circles (approximately six inches in diameter) at the areas coinciding with the chakra positions. Now, fill in these holes with circles of colored material (same type of material as the robe. I would suggest using silk throughout, though other material, such as linen, would do as well), the colors corresponding to the chakra colors/positions: red for the perineum; orange for the suprarenal; yellow for the lyden; green for the thymus; blue for the thyroid; indigo for the pineal (on the hat point); and violet for the pituitary or crown (fig. 3a). Do not simply sew the colored circles on to the uncut robe. Cut out the white circle first—in this way the color goes right through. You can also then use the cut white circle as a pattern for the colored one. An alternative to the circles, which you may prefer, is to use whole bands of color going right around the robe (fig. 3b). Do not use any other colored decoration on the robe.

When wearing the CM robe for meditation wear nothing beneath it. In this way, interference is eliminated between the colors and the body. If it is possible, do your meditation before a window (preferably open). If not, then let a white, electric incandescent light, rather than a fluorescent one, shine on you. Some people prefer to do their meditation in darkness or near darkness. If this is your preference then still follow these instructions, using the white light as a preliminary. I will later indicate how to proceed from there.

Sit comfortably, relaxing the body as much as possible, without slumping or allowing the spine to curve. Help loosen tight muscles by doing the following exercises:

Allow the head to fall forward on the chest. Breathe deeply in and out three times. Return to the upright position.

Allow the head to tip fully backward. Breathe deeply in and out three times. Return to the upright position.

Tip the head as far as possible to the left. Breathe in and out three times. Return to the upright position.

Tip the head as far as possible to the right. Breathe in and out three times. Return to the upright position.

Allow the head to fall forward, then move it in a circle, counterclockwise, three times.

Repeat the last exercise, moving the head clockwise three times. Return to the upright position.

Breathe in, through the nose, With a number of short, sharp intakes until the lungs are full. Hold it a moment, then suddenly exhale through the mouth with a *hah* sound. Do this three times.

Breathe in slowly and fully, through the right nostril (hold the left one closed, if necessary), feeling the stomach balloon out as you do so. Hold it a moment, then exhale slowly through the mouth, flattening the stomach as you do so. This exercise moves all the stale air from the bottom of the lungs. Do this three times.

Repeat the last exercise, breathing in slowly, this time through the left nostril, and out through the right nostril. Do this three times.

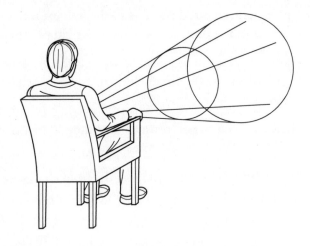

Figure 4
Cone of Light

Now, with your body relaxing and breathing normally but deeply, concentrate your thoughts until
you can imagine your whole body encased in a globe
of white light. Feel the luminous energy charging
your whole body. After a few moments of this, see
the light gradually turning to red. As it becomes red,
see it form into a cone shape, the tip of which is directed at your perineum chakra. As you continue to
breathe deeply, see and feel the red light slowly flow
into the perineum area. When you feel you have absorbed all that you can, see the all-encompassing
globe of white light return.

Next, let the white light give way to a cone of orange. The point of the cone is directed at the suprarenal (fig. 4). Again, as you breathe deeply, feel the orange light pouring down the cone and into your whole body.

Continue in this fashion, working through all the chakras and drawing all their respective colors into you. Finish with the all-encompassing white light that you had at the start. If you find it difficult to envision the different colors, set up a chart where you can see them before you. A good one can be made from rectangles of colored paper—the sort used in schools, obtainable from any stationary store—pasted on a larger black sheet (fig. 5). A glance at the chart each time sets the required color in your mind.

Having completed these preliminaries, you will now enter an incredibly deep and satisfying meditation. One of the first rewards will be tremendous peace of mind and inner satisfaction. If you prefer to meditate in reduced light, draw the blind over the window or extinguish the white light and settle back. At the end of the meditation period, before returning to normalcy, imagine yourself for a few minutes encompassed in the globe of white light.

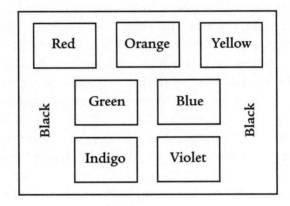

Figure 5
Color Chart for Meditating

Group Meditation

Group meditation can bring enormous satisfaction. The interaction of each person's vibrations work in a complementary manner resulting in tremendous psychic achievement. When meditating alone, you may, once in a while, experience an off day. This is never the case with group meditation. In fact, for this reason, many people will only meditate with a group.

In group meditation, I again recommend wearing the CM robe. In all meditative situations, and, as we shall see, in most other areas of occult practice, the

CM robe serves as a remarkable catalyst. The group should seat themselves in a circle and should go through their breathing and light exercises in their own time. At the completion, by everyone, of the chakra color reinforcement, the white electric light should be extinguished, or blinds drawn, and the circle should then be illuminated by a blue light. In the group with which I work, we use a Westinghouse 100-watt, color-tone floodlight. It is available just about everywhere and is ideal for the purpose. This blue light should remain on throughout the meditation.

If you already meditate and hesitate to encompass color magick in what may have become your set procedure, try this simple test. Do your meditation just as you normally would, but do it in the light of a blue bulb. I guarantee you will have one of the best meditations you have ever had!

Some final words on meditation generally. You must meditate consistently. Some say twice a day: morning and evening, for twenty minutes each period. I personally think once a day for fifteen minutes is sufficient. But, whatever you choose, be consistent. Do it the same time(s) each day and every day. Do not just do it occasionally, as the fancy strikes you.

When you first start to meditate, you will find it difficult to sit still for more than a few minutes at a time. Your body will want to fidget; you will perhaps feel a great itch developing, demanding to be scratched! It takes a little time, but you will soon become master of your physical self. Ignore the itch; however much it screams, it will go away.

Meditation should not be confused with prayer. When you pray, you petition deity. You are asking. In meditation, you are listening; perhaps you will hear the answers to your prayers. Prayer and meditation complement one another.

People who have never meditated before have said to me, "But how do you keep your mind completely blank for a quarter of an hour?"

The answer is: you do not! It would be, I think, an impossibility. No, what you do is focus your mind on a concept. In TM one is given a mantra on which to focus. A mantra is a word or sound of spiritual, frequently religious, significance that serves as a focal point for the mind while allowing the psychic centers to open up and receive what may be forthcoming. In the meditation taught by Edgar Cayce, you focus on an affirmation; a short phrase or sentence that capsulates thoughts relevant to approaches in a search for God/Goddess.

Neither mantras nor affirmations are necessary. You can dwell on any word(s) or on a symbol. If you are seeking answers to questions, then concentrate on those questions. Try to break them down to their lowest denominators, or to the fewest words possible. Study those words and see them, as it were, in your mind, in the position of the third eye. Place them there, at the pineal gland, and let your mind dwell on them. Gradually, answers will come. Perhaps not immediately, but they will come. Often, when you reach this stage, you are suddenly aware of a white light. It is both within us and about us. This does not always happen, but when it does, it is one of the most satisfying of occult experiences.

2

Color in Psychic Development

There are many people who seem, very obviously, to have ESP. The sort of people who know that the telephone is going to ring before it actually does; who know who is on the other end of the line before they pick up the receiver. These people have their psychic power developed quite naturally. Often times other people envy them, thinking, "I could never be like that. I don't have any such power." Yet that is not true. Everyone has that power. Everyone has psychic ability. It is just that in some people, as we have seen, the power comes out naturally, while in others, it has to be drawn out.

There are many different ways to draw out your psychic power. In this chapter, I will show a few of the ways to use color for psychic development. I will deal with ESP (extra sensory perception); clairvoyance (literally, *clear seeing*); clairaudience (*clear hearing*); clairsentience (*clear sensing*); psychokinesis (moving objects without physical contact); and other allied practices.

First Exercise

Take seven pieces of colored material, each in one of the seven primary colors. The pieces should all be the same size and of the same material. I use squares of colored felt. You can use whatever you like (cloth, silk, felt, construction paper, cardboard) so long as all are the same in size and material. Now, sit quietly and go through the breathing exercises detailed in chapter 1, pages 10, 11, and 12. Correct breathing is a very important part of psychic development, and these exercises should always be performed before any experiment.

Sitting at a table, close your eyes and mix up the colors in front of you. Then, take one color and, with your eyes kept closed, hold it between your hands, palm to palm. Concentrate on the material and see if you can sense (not *guess*) the color you hold. Does it feel warm, or cool? Do your palms or fingers tingle? Hold it to your forehead and to your cheek. Any different reaction? When you feel you know the color, open your eyes and check. If you are wrong, do not worry. Make a note of your choice. Take a sheet of paper and draw three columns (fig. 6). Column one should be headed **Color**. In that column, write the actual color you find yourself holding. Column two is headed **Sense**. In that column, write the color that you thought you held. Column three is **Sensations,** and there you should write any reactions you have.

Color	Sense	Sensations
Red	Red	Warm, love
Green	Violet	Pleasant, cool
Yellow		
Blue	Green	Cool, trees
Red	Orange	Heat, danger
Indigo		

Figure 6
Color Sensation Chart

For example, you might have felt the color was cool and vaguely unpleasant. Or, it might have felt warm and friendly. Write down anything you felt even if, on the face of it, it does not seem necessarily applicable to a color.

Put the color back with the rest and again close your eyes and mix them up. Go through the same procedure: mix the colors, pick up one, hold it and try to sense it, and note the results.

Keep this up for at least ten minutes, then sit back and check your results. They should prove interesting. Do not be disappointed if most of your choices were wrong. A *close* is almost as good as a *correct* (e.g., if the color was red and you thought it was orange). Examine the sensations. The red end of the color scale is the hot end; the blue is the cold. Red will stimulate, while blue will calm.

Let us examine the results of a test that was conducted with children in a school in England. The children were shown fabrics of different colors and asked to write down their feelings about these colors. This was the result:

Red: Danger. Anger. Fire. Love. Thirst. Mean. Hate.

Orange: Woods. Autumn. Warm. Kind. Fire.

Yellow: Summer. Sleep. Glad. Light. Easter. Sick.

Green: Cool. Nice. Flowers. Ocean. Picnic. Reading. Snakes.

Blue: Water. Cool. Lazy. Home. Frost. Lonely.

Indigo: Soft. Gentle. Sweet. Prayers.

Violet: Sad. Church. Love. Warmth.

I will not attempt to analyze these, but from this list you may find certain parallels with your own. It is interesting, I think, that there are one or two seeming contradictions contained in the list. For example, red stimulates both love and hate; yellow both gladness and sickness.

Traditional Associations

In the metaphysical world colors do, traditionally, have certain associations (for example, those used in candle-burning magick). The traditional associations are as follows:

Red: Strength, health, vigor, sexual love, danger, charity.

Orange: Encouragement, adaptability, stimulation, attraction, plenty, kindness.

Yellow: Persuasion, charm, confidence, jealousy, joy, comfort.

Green: Finance, fertility, luck, energy, charity, growth

Blue: Tranquility, understanding, patience, health, truth, devotion, sincerity.

Indigo: Changeability, impulsiveness, depression, ambition, dignity.

Violet: Tension, power, sadness, piety, sentimentality.

It is useful to know these associations for purposes of psychic development. This will be explained more fully later on.

Second Exercise

The transitional period between waking and sleeping is the *hypnogogic state;* between sleeping and waking is the *hypnopompic state.* Either of these times is excellent for psychic experimentation.

Try this experiment/exercise. Take seven colored pieces of material (the seven primary colors) and place each in a separate, windowed envelope. Seal the envelopes. With the windows downward, mix them up. Just before you go to bed, pick one envelope at random, and place it under your pillow, taking care that you do not see the color through the envelope window. Just as you are on the point of falling asleep, concentrate your thoughts on the envelope under the pillow, trying to pick up the color inside. There is a very simple way to do this. Lie on your back and, with your arms at your sides, raise one hand and forearm (bent at the elbow) straight up in the air. As you fall into sleep your hand and arm will fall back across you, waking you again. At that moment, try to sense the color beneath your pillow. Write it down (however roughly, and quickly!) then go to sleep.

As soon as you wake in the morning, again write down the color you then sense, along with any sensations, thoughts, or feelings associated with it. The color you sense as you wake (in the hypnopompic state) may well be different from what you sense in the hypnogogic state. Do not worry. List them both. You will need three headings on your recording sheet: **Color** (as seen through the envelope's window in the morning); **Hypnogogic** (falling asleep sensation); **Hypnopompic** (awakening sensation).

Put the envelope back with the others and mix them. Repeat the experiment the next night, and for a total of twenty-one nights. From this, as well as seeing how well you are able to pick up the colors generally, you will see which is the better time for you to do your psychic work—evening or morning.

Third Exercise

A very simple, yet effective, ESP test can be done using twelve playing cards. From a deck of regular playing cards take out the eight, nine, ten of clubs; eight, nine, ten of spades; eight, nine, ten of hearts; and the eight, nine, ten of diamonds (these are the twelve cards bearing the largest number of *pips*—most useful for differentiating between red and black, which you are going to do). Shuffle these twelve cards and then lay them, facedown, in a row on the table in front of you.

Now, going from left to right, try to sense each card as to whether it is red or black. That is all. Do not concern yourself with the actual suit, or the value; just whether it is red or black.

You may find it helpful to gently lay your fingertips on the back of each card, or, perhaps, to hold the palm of the hand over it. Experiment. Write down your guesses (senses). Then turn the cards over and see how correct you were.

Shuffle the cards and repeat the experiment. Always work from left to right. Do it ten times, at least, keeping score of your results.

Since there are only two possible answers to each guess, expect an average of six correct each run, for chance. If chance alone is at work, therefore, you will have approximately sixty correct in going through ten times. If, however, you find you have considerably more than sixty correct (or considerably less) then ESP is at work. For example, if you have seventy-three correct, the odds are twenty to one against chance; seventy-eight correct and the odds are one hundred to one against chance. Of course, the more times you go through, the more accurate a picture you will get. Here are the odds for various runs through:

Number of Runs	Chance Score	Good (20:1 against chance)	Excellent (100:1 against chance)
10	60	73	78
20	120	144	152
30	180	215	222
40	240	286	295
50	300	356	365

If you want to make the above experiment more interesting, and more of a challenge, then use photographs of people instead of playing cards: six colored photographs and six black-and-white photographs. You will probably have to put each photograph in an envelope so that they all appear the same. Try to simply differentiate between the colored and the black-and-white. It will be more difficult because, from the pictures, you will also be getting feelings, emotions, health, etc., that could be confusing. It might help a little to have all the colored photographs of women and the black-and-white photographs of men.

Fourth Exercise

Imagery is a step toward clairvoyance. Sit in a comfortable straight-backed chair. The one you use for meditation is ideal. Wear your CM robe for this experiment.

Close your eyes and do your breathing exercises. Then, after a moment's quiet, imagine that there is a large tube standing on the floor in front of you. It is like those large cardboard tubes used for mailing posters, etc. See it standing, on end, in front of you. In your mind, reach out and take the tube. Lift it up and look through it, as a child might in pretending it is a telescope. This is your psychic telescope to other worlds, other realities.

See the tube stretching away in front of you. It is large enough that you can look down it with both eyes (keep your actual eyes closed, of course). See it, in your mind's eye, stretching away off into the distance. There is no weight to it so it can stretch away for miles, if necessary. At the far end of the tube see the color green.

Now, much like with an actual telescope or the zoom lens of a movie camera, bring your tube into focus. Shorten it. Let the far end move in toward you and see that the green is now the green of grass. See a vast field of grass, perhaps with green trees off to one side. Shorten the tube again. Bring that scene in closer and closer until you can see all the details. If you want to, you can focus on just one small item, just one blade of grass.

Now, extend the tube again and let the end be the general green color. Change the green to blue. At the far end of your tube is the color blue. Gradually bring it into focus, shortening the tube. See now that the blue is a large armchair. It is in a room. See the room, and all its details. You can move the end of the tube around as you wish, getting either a general view of the whole room or closing in on a single piece of furniture or item of decoration.

In clairvoyance you can see such a room as the room of the person you wish to contact. As you look at it you can make the door open and bring whomever you wish into the room. Another way to contact a person is to go through the above procedure but, in moving back from the color, see that color as the color of the person's dress or suit. If you like, the person can be standing with their back to you initially. Once you have moved back, got them in focus, and are ready to begin, you can then get them to turn around. The tube imagery, with a color starting point, can be a very useful introduction to clairvoyance.

At the conclusion of the sitting, simply return to a single color, shorten the tube to its original size, and stand it back down on the floor in front of you. After a few moments of quiet, you can open your eyes.

Fifth Exercise

Radiesthesia (the use of a pendulum for metaphysical purposes) can be extremely effective and I will deal extensively with it in later chapters on healing. As an introduction, however, try this simple exercise. Cut a strip of white paper, or cardboard, approximately twelve inches long and one inch wide. Color one end of the strip red, about two inches of it will do, and the other end blue. A two-inch section in the center should be colored yellow.

If you have a pendulum, fine. If not, then making one is very easy. Virtually any weight on the end of a string will do. A favorite is to loop a length of silk ribbon through a ring. Even a needle on the end of a thread will do. A neck pendant on a fine chain is another possibility. The length of the thread/string/chain should be about seven to ten inches. Hold the chain between the thumb and forefinger so that, with the elbow resting on the table, the pendulum is suspended just above the table's surface. (Some radiesthesiatists suggest keeping the arm in the air, with the elbow off the table, but I have found no difference either way. Resting the elbow is certainly less tiring.) Use the right hand if right-handed, the left if left-handed.

Hold the pendulum so that it is suspended over the center of the red section of your strip of paper as it lies on the table. Hold the chain still; do not consciously try to swing the pendulum. Do not grip it too tightly. Now, concentrate your thoughts on the color red. See a ball of red light at the end of the strip of paper. See it encompassing the pendulum. You will soon notice the pendulum starting to swing. It will swing more and more strongly moving in a circle, clockwise about the red area (fig. 7).

When it is swinging well, move your arm across so that the pendulum is now suspended over the blue end. See, here, a blue ball of light encompassing the pendulum. You will probably be surprised to find that the pendulum will slow, stop, and start to swing again in the opposite, counterclockwise, direction. As much as you change ends, and color concentrations, so will the pendulum change directions. If you stop it and then hold it over the center section, and imagine yellow, it will swing backward and forward along the line of the strip of paper.

You will get the same reactions from the pendulum if, instead of simply imagining the appropriate colors, you concentrate your thoughts on those things that

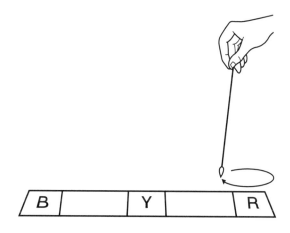

Figure 7
Using a Pendulum

are associated with the colors (see Traditional Associations, pages 23 and 24). Over red, think of strength, health, vigor, etc. Over blue, think of tranquility, understanding, and devotion. Over yellow, envision attraction, charm, and confidence.

Sixth Exercise

Psychokinesis (PK) is the moving of material objects without physical contact. To demonstrate the pressures applied in PK, we can perform a simple exercise using an animate object . . . a person. You will actually need a minimum of three people for this exercise (more than three is fine). On one side of the room sit one person (or group) that we will call A. On the other side of the room sit another person (or group) we will call B. Let a toss of the coin decide which person (or group) will be red and which blue. For the first run, let us say that A is red and B is blue.

Now, bring in a person who has been kept outside while the coin was tossed. This should be a person who is fairly relaxed. Have him or her stand in the center of the room, at ease, with the legs slightly apart. Let us call this person X.

Groups A and B should now concentrate their thoughts on their respective colors. With eyes closed, they should see themselves surrounded by red or blue light and should see it extending out to touch X. (If there are several people, so that you have groups rather than individuals, then let one or two of each group concentrate on the Traditional Associations, pages 23 and 24, rather than on the actual color.

What will (or should) happen now is that X will find him/herself being drawn toward the red group—in this first run, A—and repelled by the blue group. X will probably become aware of feelings of warmth and love coming from the red group; coldness from the blue. Do this experiment a number of times, flipping a coin each time to see which will be red and which blue. Do not, of course, let X know which is which. You will find that X will far more frequently be drawn to the red than to the blue. Question X after each run and get reactions.

Seventh Exercise

A simple exercise can be done using a cork ball (easily obtained at fishing-supply stores). Tie a length of thread to a pin and then push the pin into the cork-ball. Hang the ball so that it is free on all sides.

Point your forefinger at the suspended ball, as close as you can without actually touching it (fig. 8), and concentrate your thoughts on the color blue. Feel the blue all about you; see it about and even within your body. Direct it down your arm and out of your finger. As you direct out the blue, you should see the cork ball move away from your finger.

Concentrate on red, and the cork ball will swing toward you, actually hitting the tip of your finger. Experiment with other colors.

Eighth Exercise

Clairaudience is the ability to hear psychically. It may be accompanied by clairvoyance, but not necessarily so. How do we hear color? Through music.

Color and music share common terms. We speak of *tone, pitch, intensity,* and *volume,* for both arts. *Chromatic* is another common word. There is a psychological phenomenon whereby certain people subconsciously

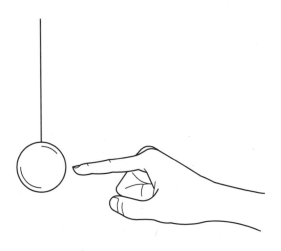

Figure 8
Psychokinesis Exercise

see colors in sounds. This is known as color synesthe-
sia. Colors can even be brought about by sound. In the
Los Angeles Times (December 3, 1948) there was an Associated Press report on a machine known as an Auro-
ratone, invented by an Englishman named Cecil Stokes.
Musical vibrations registered on a sensitized emulsion
and were photographed by a movie camera. A different
pattern of color was created in the emulsion by each
individual note. When projected, accompanied by the
music, the result was a glorious series of color patterns
subtly changing with the mood of the music. More recently, a color organ has been developed by Thomas
Douglas Jones. Known as the Chromaton, it produces
colored light as it is played.

Sir Issac Newton, three hundred years ago, related
colors to the diatonic scale: C = red; D = orange; E =
yellow; F = green; G = blue; A = indigo; B = violet. Slow
music is generally associated with the blue end of the
scale, and fast music with the red end.

An interesting exercise toward clairaudience can be
performed using a large conch shell. We are all familiar
with the *sounds of the sea* that can be heard by holding
such a shell to the ear, but more than the sea can be
heard by the sensitive.

Sit comfortably, back straight, breathing exercises done, and hold the shell to your ear. You will
first hear the familiar rushing sound but, if you
concentrate, you may become aware of a subtle musical background sound. Concentrate on it and try to

bring it out. In clairaudience a shell is often used, by a developing medium, to spark the initial contact and to focus the voice(s) being heard. If you can also pick up a musical accompaniment, as it were, then you can glean additional, useful information based on the tempo and pitch of the music, together with any repeated, emphasized, individual notes, This is not easy to do, admittedly, but you might take heart from the fact that some years ago, Theodore F. Karwoski and Henry S. Odbert conducted a study* with 148 people, testing for color response to music. Of these, 60 percent did get a response of some kind (40 percent of these actually *saw* colors). If you get that sort of response then, again, refer to the color associations listed in Tradional Associations, pages 23 and 24.

Color-Music, Psychological Monographs Vol. 50, No. 2. 1938. Ohio State University, Columbus.

These are some simple exercises in psychic development associated with color. There are many more. Experiment yourself. Color can be a tremendously useful tool, as you will discover more and more in succeeding chapters.

Always go through the breathing exercises before any experiment. In fact, it certainly will not hurt you to do a complete color meditation each time! And remember . . . practice makes perfect.

3

Color in Divination

There are many different methods of divination. Some people prefer cards, others crystal- or mirror-gazing, still others work with numerology or the I Ching. Over the centuries there has been an incredible variety of forms of divination, many with unpronounceable names: alectoromancy, astragalomancy, oneiromancy, moleosophy, tasseography, libanomancy, pyromancy, molybdomancy, cephalomancy, lampadomancy, and so on. But whatever the form, and whatever the label, there are really only two criteria: Is it accurate? Does it work for you?

To help you find a method that does work for you, and one that you will feel comfortable with, and especially to improve accuracy, you can use the principles of color.

The actual basics of how to divine (how to read the Tarot, how to crystal-gaze, how to work a pendulum, etc.) I have dealt with elsewhere* so, concentrating on the advantages of color in divination, let me start out here by first looking at the place of divination. Of course, you can divine almost anywhere—spread out your Tarot cards in the sand at the beach, or throw the I Ching sticks in the back of a pickup truck—but if you are serious about this art, if you want to get the very best of results and get them consistently, then you will find it pays to be more selective.

The Divination Room

A divination room is the ideal; one set aside just for divining. This may be asking too much, however, particularly if you only have a two-room apartment! So the next ideal is the divination cabinet. Spiritualist mediums frequently operate from a curtained-off "tent" arrangement known as a *cabinet*. It serves a very useful purpose in containing whatever energies are raised. A variation of the spiritualist cabinet can serve you, but where the medium's is invariably black yours will be colored. It is no coincidence, by the way,

---

A Pocket Guide to the Supernatural Raymond Buckland. Ace Books, New York, 1969 and *Secrets of Gypsy Fortuntelling*, Llewellyn Publications, St. Paul, 1988.

that many *fortunetellers* at carnivals, in Gypsy tea rooms, or working out of storefronts, do their actual readings in colorful curtained-off areas.

The ideal cabinet should be just large enough to contain two chairs and a card table. It should be roofed; the height no more than six feet. (It is not difficult to design a wooden framework that will fold down to handy carrying size, thereby making your cabinet portable.) The actual color(s) of the drapes enclosing the framework will be a matter of experimentation. The obvious choice would seem to be blue: tranquility, understanding, patience, truth, etc. (see Traditional Associations, pages 23 and 24), but there are other possibilities. You may find that the joy and comfort of yellow, or the stimulation and attraction of orange, or the power of violet, are more condusive to your doing readings. Why not a combination of colors? Two sides of blue, two of green, and a roof of yellow might be an ideal combination. I find that the cooler colors are more sympathetic to the wide variety of readings you are likely to encounter than are the hotter ones.

To find the best color(s) for you to work under, without spending lots of dollars on yards and yards of different materials, test yourself with colored lights. Do a few divinatory layouts in blue light, then a few in green light, and so on. Note that I say a few *layouts,* not *readings.* With many forms of divination—the Tarot is, perhaps, the most obvious—color plays a part in the interpretation. With everything bathed in a blue light, then, all your colors would be affected. So, at this stage, do not try to do any actual readings/interpretations, just get the feeling of working in that color light.

You will find that there are one, two, or perhaps three colors that leave you far more relaxed than the others. Then this color/color combination is the one you will use to cover your cabinet. It sets the right vibrations for you to work in. A candle, or desk lamp on the table can then take care of the illumination for the actual readings, and so overcome the lighting problem mentioned above.

Now to specifics. How can color improve the accuracy of scrying? What does color have to do with numerology? What color is the I Ching? What about color and palmistry? There are many ways that color can improve these, and most other, forms of divination.

Crystal-Gazing

Crystal-gazing, a branch of scrying, is a form, of divination that many people have trouble with. Usually it is just a question of practice, but many get discouraged before they achieve their first vision.

Instead of just gazing into the crystal and hoping for something (anything!) to appear, start out with a definite objective in mind. Do your breathing exercises, as detailed in chapter 1 (I would also recommend wearing the CM robe, not only for this particular exercise, but for all the experiments outlined in this book). Then, sit quietly and focus your mind on what you would like to see. Perhaps you have a particular question you want answered, or a specific person you want to see. Boil down that question, or person, to a single point: an emotion, a feeling, or an action.

For example, you would like to meet with your recently deceased, greatly missed, Uncle Max. He was always a jolly person, full of vigor, seemingly healthy, which was why everyone was surprised when he suddenly dropped dead in the middle of the church picnic. *Vigor* would seem to sum up Uncle Max (vigor = red).

For a second example, you would like to find out whether the weekend meditation seminar you plan to attend will be beneficial and how it will affect you. This is basically a combination of tranquility/devotion and need for understanding, all of which are allied with the color blue.

Take the color you have arrived at and, in your mind, project it into the crystal ball. See the ball full of that color (blue, or red, or whatever). Do not try to project Uncle Max himself in there, or a full weekend seminar. It would be too complicated and would defeat its own objective. No, just project the color. Proceed as normal and you will find that when the scene finally *breaks* it will be centered on the person/question you wanted.

If you have difficulty projecting a color into the ball with your mind, slip a small square of the appropriately colored velvet, or silk, underneath the ball. With this method, however, you must remove the cloth once the imagery starts. Try to carefully slip the material out again from under the ball (and drop it on the floor, or put it behind you on the chair). Be warned, it will be difficult to do this without losing concentration and, hence, the whole picture. The reason the colored cloth must be removed is that the color permeation could interfere with other color information that is to come to you.

Much of what you see in a crystal (or in any other form of scrying: mirror, inkblot, water, polished copper, etc.) is symbolic, as in most methods of divination. Pick up on colors as much as you can, and use the Traditional Associations, pages 23 and 24, to help you interpret.

Numerology and Chromology

Numerology may seem a far cry from chromology but the two can usefully be put together. The key is in the numerical value of the primary colors. They are as follows:

1—Red

2—Orange

3—Yellow

4—Green

5—Blue

6—Indigo

7—Violet

8—Rose

9—Gold

To equate seven primary colors with nine primary numbers, it is necessary to go into the higher octave for the colors, i.e., rose is the higher octave of red; gold is the higher octave of orange. Rose and gold, then, have similar associations to those equated with red and orange in the Traditional Associations, pages 23 and 24. Rose = strength, love, leadership, judgment, arbitration, and respect. Gold = joy, cheer, hope, happiness, communication, and counseling.

From basic numerology we have the numerical values of the letters of the alphabet:

1	=	A	J	S
2	=	B	K	T
3	=	C	L	U
4	=	D	M	V
5	=	E	N	W
6	=	F	O	X
7	=	G	P	Y
8	=	H	Q	Z
9	=	I	R	

As an example, let us look at ex-President Jimmy Carter through numerology/chromology. Remember that in numerology you work with the name most commonly used, so it is Jimmy Carter, not James Carter.

J	I	M	M	Y	C	A	R	T	E	R
1	9	4	4	7	3	1	9	2	5	9 =

$$54 \ (5 + 4) = 9$$

Note the preponderance of 9's. There are three in the names and then the name number itself is a 9. In numerology, a 9 person is very emotional; active, though ruled by the emotions; tied very much to family background; impulsive. Okay. But what more can we learn by chromology? Well, 9 is the number of gold, and gold means joy, cheer, happiness (that ever-present, toothy smile?), hope, communication and counseling.

You can go a step further. With the three 9's in the name there are also two 1's (red) and two 4's (green). This would then indicate strength, vigor, charity; growth, energy, and luck.

There is one further step you can take: what is lacking? All numbers are represented with the exception of 6 (indigo) and 8 (rose). We can ignore the absence of 8 since there are a couple of 1's, and we know that 8 is simply a higher octave of 1. So the only number/color totally absent is 6 (indigo), a color associated with dignity. It might, then, behoove Mr. Carter to wear the color indigo, perhaps in a tie, in order to give his appearance more dignity and generally round himself out chromologically. So, from this example, it can be seen that chromology can indeed expand on basic numerological insight.

Rolling Dice

A step along from numerology is divining with dice. A very basic, simple method, useful to determine the outcome of events or the choice of a path to take, is to have the querant roll a pair of dice. The resultant individual numbers, plus their sum, are then equated with colors as in numerology.

For example, suppose the querant wishes to know whether or not she should meet with a certain man on a particular weekend. She concentrates her thoughts on the question as she handles the dice, then throws them down. Let us say they land showing a 2 and a 5. We know that 2 is orange and 5 is blue. The sum of the two numbers is 7—violet.

From the Traditional Associations listed on pages 23 and 24, you can interpret. Orange gives encouragement, stimulation, attraction. Blue shows understanding, devotion, sincerity . . . it sounds good for that weekend. Violet, the sum of the two, shows sentimentality but also tension, possibly sadness. From the positivity of the orange and blue you can probably ignore the sadness, or soft-pedal it. The tension is certainly understandable, and not necessarily a bad thing. To sum up, you could say that the weekend promises to be very productive. There will be good rapport, perhaps after an initial uneasiness.

This form of divination can, obviously, be expanded to other branches, such as dealing out playing cards, or overturning dominoes. The basic interpretation will rest on equating the resultant numbers with colors.

An expansion of the above would be a form of astragalomancy. This was the name given to divining by a letter, or symbol, on each of twelve knucklebones thrown down on the ground. Variations are found all over the world: the natives in Nigeria use six carved pieces of wood; the Shoshone Indians use different shaped stones. Interpretation depends upon how and where the objects fall.

Take three wooden cubes, each about the size of a regular die. On each cube/die paint one side red, one side orange, one yellow, one green, one blue, and one violet.

The querant places a coin on the ground, to represent him- or herself. He or she then shakes up the three colored dice, concentrating his or her thoughts on the question. The dice are thrown down on the coin. Interpretation is of the resultant colors according to their relationship to the coin—the closer a color to the coin, the more powerful and immediate the force(s) affecting the individual. It will be found that many times two, or even all three, of the dice will show the same color, indicating very powerful and positive influences.

Tarot

When teaching the Tarot, I have always emphasized
that the Tarot cards should be interpreted according to the reader's *feelings* rather than by reading off
specific meanings from a published book of *interpretations*. If a particular card—let us say the Ten of
Wands, for illustration—turns up in a particular
position when you are reading for person A, then it
has certain meanings for that person. But, if that
same Ten of Wands should show up in the same
position in a reading for person B, then it is not
likely to have the self-same meaning; for A and B
are two separate and very distinct personalities.

Reading from a typical Tarot book, the meaning for
the Ten of Wands is given as "overcoming a problem;
sweeping away opposition; assertion." Going from
such a book, that is all the card means; the meaning is
applied to persons A, B, C, and so on. I do not believe it
can apply to all and sundry. Throw away that book!

As you turn over each card, your eyes will be drawn
to a specific symbol, a particular part or aspect of the
illustration far more strongly than to any other part.
This is the key to your interpretation—not what a
book says.

I want to bring out the point that your eye will not
only be attracted by a particular object or symbol, but
also that it will pick up one particular color more
than the others. This *color consciousness* can be very
useful in adding interpretations of what you see.

The Waite-Rider deck is an excellent one, and one I personally use regularly. When I wish to work more with chromology in my readings, however, I find that the best is the Crowley-Thoth deck. Concentrate on the color vibrations, and see what a lift it will give to your readings.

Color, then, can play a very useful part in divination. I have given some suggested uses; there are many more you will find for yourself.

Instead of throwing the I Ching sticks (or coins) on a table or a rug, lay down a square of material of a color appropriate to the question being asked.

When reading palms, be aware of any warmth or coldness—especially at the fingertips and on the mounds—and equate these with the red and blue ends of the color spectrum.

In radiesthesia, try using different colored pendula. Experiment for yourself.

4

Color in Magick

Aleister Crowley defined magick as "the art or science of causing change to occur in conformity with will." In simpler terms he was saying, "Make something happen that you want to happen." That is magick. I do not think that definition can be bettered. Color magick, then, is making something you want to happen, do so, through the use of color.

What sorts of things do people want to have happen? We can usually divide up our wishes and desires under four main headings: health, wealth, power, and protection.

Anything we desire, can be. Anything. The power is ours. Here follows some simple rituals using color magick, which can help us draw on our own powers to create our own realities. Work them in quiet solitude* when there is a real need (do not attempt magick simply *to see if it will work*). A word of caution—you can create your own reality, but do not do it by interfering with someone else's reality. An example would be love magick to influence a particular person. This should never be done, for it would be interfering with their free will; forcing them to do something they would not normally do, and might not want to do. The only sort of love magick that should be done is that aimed non-specifically . . . to bring *someone* to you, without knowing exactly who it will be. Far better to work on yourself, to make yourself generally more attractive, than to try to change someone else. So, always consider what effect your magick might have on others.

---

*By which I mean cut off from the ordinary everyday world . . . preferably in a room kept aside solely for magickal purposes. The rituals themselves may be done by the individual or by a group.

Incense should always be burned throughout the magickal ritual. Apart from helping give the right atmosphere, it is said that the smoke of the incense carries your prayers up to the gods. Any pleasant-smelling incense will do. I would particularly recommend frankincense or sandalwood, but follow your own preference. Cones, stick, or powdered incenses are equally suitable.

Most magickal rituals are best performed after sundown but, again, choose the time most convenient for yourself. What matters is that you should be comfortable as you work. You should be comfortable as regards time, place (feeling that you will be completely free from any interruptions), and your dress. Again, I would recommend the CM robe, with nothing beneath it.

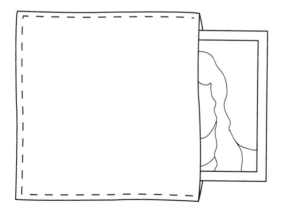

Figure 9
Placket

These rituals may be done for yourself or for another. In the rituals you will be using colored plackets. *Placket* is the old English word for *pocket* (it was also a slang term for the vagina). These are simple pockets made by sewing together two rectangles of colored material, leaving one side open so that an object, such as a photograph, may be inserted (fig. 9). I made my plackets of felt, but silk, cotton, or just about any material will do. I have plackets in each of the primary colors, plus one healing placket that is red on one side and green on the other, and others in combinations of colors (e.g., green and blue for *to bring good fortune*—see below).

A tabletop, shelf, or top of a chest-of-drawers can be set up as an altar. On it you should have a religious

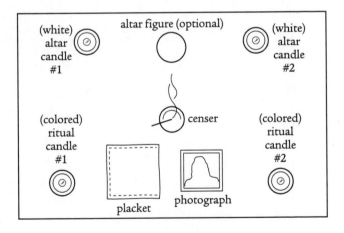

Figure 10
Altar

figure/symbol/picture (if you so desire; this is optional), with a white altar candle on either side of it. Your censer (incense dish) is in front of these. To the left and the right are your colored ritual candles (see below), with the placket in between (fig. 10). For working the following rituals I have indicated that photographs of the recipients be inserted in the plackets. If a photograph is not available, then use any representation of that person (e.g., an object belonging to the person that has been handled by them, such as a handkerchief; a specimen of their handwriting; a small poppet†; or, if nothing else, their full name and birth date written on a piece of paper.

---

†Magical doll—see chapter 5.

To Bring Health to Someone Sick

(See also chapters 6 and 7.)
Ritual candles 1 and 2 should be red. Placket should
be red and green.

Light altar candles 1 and 2.
Light incense.

Spend a few minutes in quiet meditation, preparing your mind for the ritual. If you wish, you may say
the Lord's Prayer (or other prayer, suitable to your
persuasion).

Petitioner Speaks

I am here to bring renewed health
to . . . (name) . . .
through the powers that be,
working their will through me,
I would bring about a body and
mind fit and well;
healed of all infirmities and
happy and joyous in life and love.

Light ritual candles 1 and 2.
Take up photograph of recipient and
hold it in the smoke of the incense.

"Here is . . . (name) . . .
    This is he/she.

Place the photograph in placket and then hold placket between the palms of the hands. Concentrate your thoughts on recipient. See him/her well and happy‡. See the power of light—the red light of health and strength, and the green light of energy, growth, and healing—flowing down, through your body, and into the recipient. Keep this up for as long as you can concentrate, then lay the placket back down on the altar.

Clear your mind and see, now, a ball of white light filling the room, purifying everything and everyone within it. According to your preference, you may say either the Twenty-third Psalm or the Pagan Seax-Wica Psalm.

23rd Psalm

The Lord is my shepherd; I shall not want.
He maketh me to lie down in green pastures:
    he leadeth me beside the still waters.
He restoreth my soul: he leadeth me in the paths
    of righteousness for his name's sake.

Yea, though I walk through the valley of
    the shadow of death, I will fear no

---

‡If the recipient has a broken leg, see him or her running and jumping; if the recipient has a sore throat, see him or her shouting and singing; if a bad back, see him or her turning somersaults! In other words, see the recipient in pefect health; not *getting* better, but *already* better.

evil: for thou art with me; thy rod
and thy staff they comfort me.
Thou preparest a table before me
in the presence of mine enemies:
thou anointest my head with oil;
my cup runneth over.
Surely goodness and mercy
shall follow me all the days of my life
and I will dwell in the
house of the Lord forever.

Seax-Wica Psalm

Ever as I pass through the ways
do I feel the presence of the gods.
I know that in aught I do
they are with me.
They abide in me
and I in them,
forever.
No evil shall be entertained,
for purity is the dweller
within me and about.
For good do I strive
and for good do I live.
Love unto all things,
so be it, forever.

Extinguish the candles—ritual candles first, then the altar candles. Leave the photograph in the placket. If the whole altar setup can be left intact, all the better. Leave until the same hour next day, then, taking the photograph out of the placket, repeat the entire ritual.

Repeat again on the third day, then leave the photograph in the placket until the recipient is completely well.

To Bring Good Fortune

(Start this ritual on a Wednesday.)
Ritual candles should be green. Placket should be green and blue.

Light altar candles.
Light incense.

Spend a few moments in quiet meditation, preparing your mind for the ritual. If you wish, you may say the Lord's Prayer (or other prayer).

Petitioner Speaks
... (name) ...
has been as a stranger to good fortune.
Whatever the reason
may it now be meet

that the forces may change.
Let all that is good be his/her
lot from henceforth.
Let new life flow that he/she may partake
of the joys and rewards of this life,
from this day forth.

Light ritual candles.
Take up photograph of recipient and
hold it in the smoke of the incense.

Here is . . . (name) . . .
This is he/she.

Place photograph in placket and then hold plack-et between the palms of the hands. Concentrate your thoughts on recipient. See him/her happy and con-tented. See the power of light—the green light of luck and good fortune and the blue light of patience and truth—flowing down, through your body, and into the recipient. Keep this up for as long as you can con-centrate, then lay the placket back down on the altar.

Clear your mind and see, now, a ball of white light filling the room, purifying everything and everyone within it. According to your preference, you may say either the Twenty-third Psalm or the Seax-Wica Psalm (see above). Then extinguish the candles—ritual can-dles first, then the altar candles. Leave the photograph in the placket. Leave until the same hour next day, then, taking the photograph out of the placket, repeat the entire ritual.

Repeat again on the third day, then leave the photograph in the placket for seven days.

To Bring Needed Wealth§

(Start this ritual on a Wednesday.)
Ritual candles should be orange.
Placket should be green.

Light altar candles.
Light incense.

Spend a few moments in quiet meditation, preparing your mind for the ritual. If you wish, you may say the Lord's Prayer (or other prayer).

Petitioner Speaks

Great is the need of . . . (name) . . .
he/she has striven and
labored long and hard
in search of that which is needed
so desperately.
The need is great,
the desire is here.
Grant that those forces that

---

§This ritual will not bring money just for the sake of having money. It will not keep you comfortably so that you will not have to work. But if there is a need—if you have done all you possibly can, and failed, then here is magick *to bring needed wealth.*

must come into play will do so,
to bring about just ends for . . . (name) . . .

Light ritual candles.
Take up photograph of recipient and
hold it in the smoke of the incense.

Here do I present . . . (name) . . .

Place photograph in placket and then hold placket
between the palms of the hands. Concentrate your
thoughts on the recipient. See him or her holding the
necessary money in hand. See the power of light—the
green light of finance—flowing down, through your
body, and into the recipient. Keep this up for as long
as you can concentrate, then lay the placket back
down on the altar.

Clear your mind and see, now, a ball of white light
filling the room, purifying everything and everyone
within it. You may say either the Twenty-third Psalm
or the Seax-Wica Psalm (see above). Then extinguish
the candles—ritual candles first, then the altar candles. Leave the photograph in the placket. Leave until
the same hour next day, then, taking the photograph
out, repeat the entire ritual. Repeat again on the third
day, then leave the photograph in the placket for
seven days.

To Bring Happiness

Ritual candles should be orange.
Placket should be yellow.

Light altar candles.
Light incense.

Spend a few moments in quiet meditation, preparing your mind for the ritual. If you wish you may say the Lord's Prayer (or other prayer).

Petitioner Speaks

I am here to help
channel happiness to . . . (name) . . .
one who is presently without
that vivid spark of life.
I would bring a smile to his/her face
and laughter to his/her heart,
in all that he/she might do.

Light ritual candles.
Take up photograph of recipient and
hold it in the smoke of the incense.

Here is . . . (name) . . . ,
The one for whom I speak.

Place photograph in placket and then hold plack-et between the palms of the hands. Concentrate your thoughts on recipient. See him/her happy and contented in all things. See the power of light—the yellow light of joy, happiness, and comfort—flowing down, through your body, and into the recipient. Keep this up for as long as you can concentrate, then lay the placket back down on the altar.

Clear your mind and see, now, a ball of white light filling the room, purifying everything and everyone within it. You may say either the Twenty-third Psalm or the Seax-Wica Psalm (see above). Then extinguish the candles—ritual candles first, then the altar can-dles. Leave the photograph in the placket. Leave until the same hour next day, then, taking the photograph out, repeat the entire ritual.

Repeat again on the third day, then leave the pho-tograph in the placket for nine days.

To Cause Love Between Two People

(Start this ritual on a Friday.)
Ritual candles should be red. Placket should be red and orange.

Light altar candles.
Light incense.

Spend a few moments in quiet meditation, preparing your mind for the ritual. If you wish you may say the Lord's Prayer (or other prayer).

Petitioner Speaks
Let the light of love pour forth
equally between . . . (name) . . .
and another.
I am here to direct that light,
in purity and truth,
that it might attract and
seal them together
in perfect harmony of life and love;
heart to heart
and mind to mind.

Light ritual candles.
Take up photograph of the
one seeking love and
hold it in the smoke of the incense.

Here do I present . . . (name) . . .
who would be as one with another.

Place photograph in placket and then hold placket between the palms of the hands. Concentrate your thoughts on recipient. See him/her with another, both together, loving, happy, and affectionate. See the power of light—the red light of love and strength and the orange light of attraction, stimulation, adaptability, and kindness—flowing down, through your body, and into the recipient's. Keep this up for as long as you can concentrate, then lay the placket back down on the altar.

Clear your mind and see, now, a ball of white light filling the room, purifying everything and everyone within it. You may say either the Twenty-third Psalm or the Seax-Wica Psalm (see above). Then extinguish the candles—ritual candles first, then the altar candles. Leave the photograph in the placket. Leave until the same hour next day, then, taking the photograph out, repeat the entire ritual. Repeat again on the third day, then leave the photograph in the placket for twenty-one days.

To Bring Love to Fulfillment (Sex)

(Start this ritual on a Friday.)
Ritual candles should be red.
Placket should be red.

Light altar candles.
Light incense.

Spend a few moments in quiet meditation, preparing your mind for the ritual. If you wish you may say the Lord's Prayer (or other prayer).

Petitioner Speaks
That the love that exists by . . . (name) . . .
should be brought to fruition
is the desire of this petitioner.
I would bring about the physical union
of these two people,
in joy and in love;
in trust and in devotion.

*Light ritual candles.
Take up photographs of both recipients*[||]
and hold them in the smoke of the incense.

Here are . . . (name) . . . and . . . (name)
to be brought together in the joys of love.

Place photographs in placket and then hold placket between the palms of the hands. Concentrate your thoughts on recipients. See them in the act of love. See the power of light—the red light of sexual love—flowing down, through your body, and into the recipients. Keep this up for as long as you can concentrate, then lay the placket back down on the altar.

[||]If the petitioner is actually one of the recipients, e.g., if he or she is the one who wishes to consummate love with his partner—then he or she may work with just the photograph of this partner.

Clear your mind and see, now, a ball of white light filling the room, purifying everything and everyone within it. You may say either the Twenty-third Psalm or the Seax-Wica Psalm (see above). Then extinguish the candles—ritual candles first, then the altar candles. Leave the photographs in the placket. Leave until the same hour next day, then, taking the photographs out, repeat the entire ritual.

Repeat again on the third day, then leave the photographs in the placket for twenty-one days.

To Consecrate a Talisman#

(Start this ritual on the day appropriate to the purpose of the talisman—Friday for a love talisman; Wednesday for a money talisman; Saturday for a protective talisman.)

Ritual candles and placket should be colors appropriate to the purpose of the talisman (see Traditional Associations, pages 23 and 24).

Light altar candles.
Light incense.

Spend a few moments in quiet meditation, preparing your mind for the ritual. If you wish, you may say the Lord's Prayer (or other prayer).

#See chapter 5 for instructions on making a talisman.

Petitioner Speaks

I am here to consecrate this talisman.
Let it be imbued with all the power
I would have it possess.
Let that power be forever with its bearer,
focusing through this object
to enhance and magnify
his/her natural elements,
wherein he/she may use it.

Light ritual candles.
Take up talisman and
hold it in the smoke of the incense.

By the smoke of this incense do I
cleanse this talisman of all impurities,
preparing it for the reception of its
own awesome power.

Place talisman in placket and then hold placket
between the palms of the hands. Concentrate your
thoughts on the talisman, seeing it as the holder of
all power for the good of love, protection, and wealth.
See the power of the light—the red light of love,
health, and strength (or, again, whatever color/attrib-
utes you are working for)—flowing down through
your body and into the talisman. Keep this up for as

long as you can concentrate, then lay the placket back down on the altar.

Clear your mind and see, now, a ball of white light filling the room, purifying everything and everyone within it. You may say either the Twenty-third Psalm or the Seax-Wica Psalm (see above). Then extinguish the candles—ritual candles first, then the altar candles. Leave the talisman in the placket. Leave until the same hour next day, then, taking the talisman out, repeat the entire ritual. Repeat again on the third day, then leave the talisman in the placket for twenty-one days.

To Protect Against Evil

(Start this ritual on a Saturday.)
Ritual candles should be white.
Placket should be blue and violet.

Light altar candles.
Light incense.

Spend a few moments in quiet meditation, preparing your mind for the ritual. If you wish, you may say the Lord's Prayer (or other prayer).

Petitioner Speaks
Evil shall not touch upon . . . (name) . . .
for he/she shall be protected by the

all-encompassing power of light.
Let that light so shine that
naught that is evil may enter the
sphere of his/her being,
but be rejected and sent into
the everlasting darkness.

Light ritual candles.
Take up photograph of recipient and
hold it in the smoke of the incense.

Here do I present . . . (name) . . . ,
in purity.

Place photograph in placket and then hold placket
between the palms of the hands. Concentrate your
thoughts on recipient. See him/her surrounded by
the shining while light of purity, ever protected from
evil of any kind. See the power of light—the blue light
of patience, truth, and devotion, and the violet light
of power and piety . . . see them both further en-
veloped in the great white light of purity and protection—flowing down, through your body, and into the
recipient. Keep this up for as long as you can concentrate, then lay the placket back down on the altar.

Clear your mind and see, now, a ball of white light
filling the room, purifying everything and everyone
within it. You may say either the Twenty-third Psalm

or the Seax-Wica Psalm (see above). Then extinguish
the candles—ritual candles first, then the altar candles.
Leave the photograph in the placket. Leave until the
same hour next day, then, taking the photograph out,
repeat the entire ritual.

Repeat again on the third day, then leave the photograph in the placket for seven days.

To Drive out Evil Influences (Exorcise)

(Start this ritual on a Saturday.)
Ritual candles should be violet.
Placket should be white.

Light altar candles.
Light incense.

Spend a few moments in quiet meditation, preparing your mind for the ritual. If you wish, you may say
the Lord's Prayer (or other prayer).

Petitioner Speaks
I seek to cleanse and purify . . . (name) . . .
of aught that is evil
abiding within or about him/her.
Let only good enter in and
let purity abound.

Drive out and exorcise those forces
that are not one with the light,
that the gods may hold
true dominion over all.

Light ritual candles.
Take up photograph of recipient and
hold it in the smoke of the incense.

Here is . . . (name) . . .
that I seek to purify.

Place photograph in placket and then hold placket between the palms of the hands. Concentrate your thoughts on recipient. See him/her in an attitude of prayer and devotion, with white light radiating from within. See the power of light—the white light of purity, goodness, and truth—flowing down, through your body, and into the recipient. Keep this up for as long as you can concentrate, then lay the placket back down on the altar.

Clear your mind and see, now, a ball of white light filling the room, purifying everything and everyone within it. You may say either the Twenty-third Psalm or the Seax-Wica Psalm (see above). Then extinguish the candles—ritual candles first, then the altar candles. Leave the photograph in the placket. Leave until the same hour next day; then, taking the photograph out, repeat the entire ritual.

Repeat again on the third day, then leave the photograph in the placket for twenty-one days.

It can be seen that the above rituals may be adapted for many purposes. The basic, essential parts are as follows: a statement of purpose; a cleansing and naming (in the incense); a concentration of power, through the direction of (colored) light.

As with all magick, we all have this power within us, to use as we will. Through the use of color, take that power and direct it, working for the good of your fellow man and woman.

5

Advanced Color Magick

Magick is a practice. Anyone can do (or attempt to do) magick. That makes them a Magician. You do not have to be a Witch, or a practitioner of voodoo, or an oriental master to do magick. Anyone can be a Magician. Of course, some are far more successful at it than others.

There are many different forms of magick . . . dozens, perhaps even hundreds. In the previous chapter we looked at just one, placket magick—an easy and safe method. Some of the others can be very dangerous. Ceremonial magick, for example, where the

Magician is conjuring and working with various entities, most of them decidedly antagonistic toward the Magician. Not only is this dangerous but, to my mind, the risks are totally unnecessary. It is a little like trying to hook up a 1,000 volt power line to run a transistor radio! Wxhy take the risk when a simple little battery will do the job just as well and without the danger?

As I said at the start of chapter 4, magick is making something happen that you want to happen. One of the ways to do that is by building power, within a consecrated circle, and then releasing it. The power builds up in the form of a cone and is, in fact, referred to as *the cone of power* in Witchcraft. Singing, dancing, chanting, physical activity (such as sex), can all be used as ways of cultivating that power. Here is where color can come in handy. Obviously, in one chapter I cannot teach you all the intricacies of working the many different systems of magick, but I will try to show you how color can be advantageously employed in some of the systems.

Color Cone

To be an effective magickal practitioner, you need to be well versed in the arts of meditation, concentration, and visualization. Before starting your magickal work, sit for a moment and meditate on what you wish to achieve. Then, visualize the circle filling with white light. See the light all around you, totally encompassing you. It will form around you and build up into the shape of a cone. This is the white light of protection. Now, once that light is firmly there, gradually change that whiteness into a color first of pale blue, for tranquility, understanding, and sincerity. Then, gradually darken the blue. Change it to indigo and then on through to a deep purple. You will by then feel that there is already power in the circle. Keep the purple for a few moments then, gradually, change the color to the one most suitable for the magick you are going to work. If you are going to do a healing, then green might be appropriate (though, again, it will vary depending upon the type of healing). If you are working to bring money, then orange, or gold, for attraction, might be appropriate. Working for love? A pink cone would be good. Now go on to do the ritual work; the raising of the power by whatever method.

Color Carrier Beam

When the time to release the power comes, again incorporate color. Instead of just releasing, and seeing the power fly from you to its target, send it in a beam of colored light. This would be the same color as that used at the finale of the opening cone (above) . . . green for healing, orange for money, etc. When the energy has gone and you have done all you can, then return to a white cone about you.

Candle Magick

While not the subject of this book, the burning of colored candles is one of the most effective ways of working magick. I have dealt fully with this in a companion volume to the present work—*Practical Candle-burning Rituals* (Llewellyn Publications, 1982). Candle burning is perhaps the easiest way for the beginner to get into the working of magick and, especially, to become familiar with the symbolism of colors. It is another version of sympathetic magic and, again, is a safe, basic form of magick.

Poppet Magick

A *poppet* is a specially prepared cloth doll that represents a particular person. The basis of poppet magick is the sympathetic variety already discussed. Whatever you do to the doll, in ritual, you in effect do to the person it represents.

The color of the cloth you use for the doll is determined by the purpose of the poppet. Many poppets are made for healing purposes and the color will depend on the patient's problem. Refer to the Traditional Associations, pages 23 and 24, to determine the color for your poppet. You want to get a new job? Why not use indigo, the color of ambition? You are trying to develop charm and confidence? Use yellow. You want to attract money to you? Do one side of the poppet in orange (for attraction) and the other in green (for finance). Do not be afraid to have a multi-colored poppet. And use the brightest colors that you can.

From the cloth, cut out two simple, basic shapes (fig. 11). As you cut, concentrate on the person the doll is to represent. It does not have to look exactly like the person when it is done, so long as you really concentrate and, to you, the poppet actually becomes the person. Sew the two pieces of cloth together, leaving an opening in the top of the head (fig. 12).

Stuff the poppet with suitable filling. If you are doing a healing, then the appropriate herb should be used. If you are working for money, chop up some Monopoly money and stuff it with that. For love? Fill it with rose petals or confetti.

Think about a good filling. See just how creative you can be. When filled, sew up the top of the head.

Now, again concentrating hard on the actual person, decorate the poppet to look as much like the person as possible. Sew on colored wool (or real hair, if you can get it) to represent the person's hair. Embroider or draw with felt-tip pens, if you are not very good with a needle—the facial features. On the body write the person's name and mark their astrological Sun sign, Moon sign, and Rising sign, if known (fig. 13).

When writing the name, I suggest doing it in one of the traditional magickal alphabets and also doing it in the color appropriate for the person's birth date:

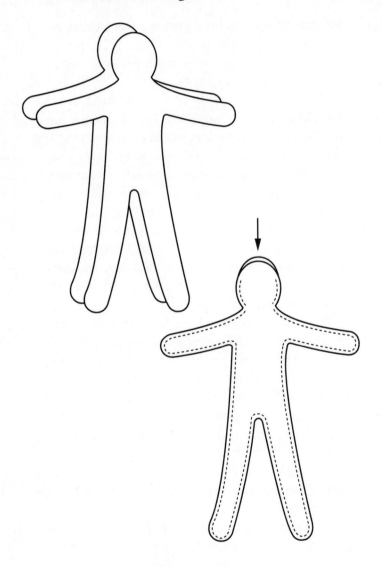

Figures 11 and 12
Poppet Construction

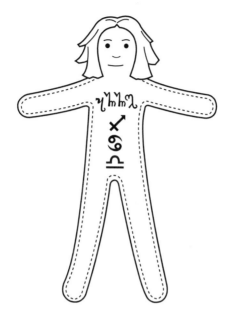

Figure 13
Completed Poppet

Aries: Red

Leo: Orange

Sagittarius: Purple

Taurus: Yellow

Virgo: Violet

Capricorn: Blue

Gemini: Violet

Libra: Yellow

Aquarius: Indigo

Cancer: Green

Scorpio: Red

Pisces: Indigo

When you have constructed your poppet, and personalized it, then it is time to begin the actual magickal ritual. You should set up an altar, as described in chapter 4, but with the poppet lying where the placket was. After lighting the candles and the incense, take up the poppet and hold it over the altar.

Say:

Here is . . . (name) . . .
This is her/him in every way.
All that I do to this poppet I do to her/him.

Hold the poppet in the smoke of the incense and see the person it represents. Proceed then as you did for the placket magick in chapter 4, but using the poppet instead of the placket/photograph.

The advantage of poppet magick is that you put so much of yourself, of your personal power, into the making of the poppet that it becomes a very potent tool.

Figure 14
Theban Alphabet

Talismans

A *talisman* is a man-made object endowed with magickal powers, especially for averting evil from, or for bringing luck to, its owner. In this sense a rosary, crucifix, St. Christopher medal, etc., are all talismans. But the most powerful magick is that done by the person affected. In the same way, the most powerful talisman is one actually made by the person who needs it. A talisman made by one person for another can never be as strong as a personally made one.

According to the magickal order, the Hermetic Order of the Golden Dawn, a talisman is "a magickal figure charged with the force that it is intended to represent." It is so charged by (1) inscription, and (2) consecration. It can be of any shape, but let us first look at the material of the talisman.

A talisman can be of virtually any material—paper, silver, copper, lead—but traditionally some substances are more appropriate than others and their use will imbue the talisman with more power. For example, as you know the days of the week are each ruled by a planet: Sunday—Sun; Monday—Moon; Tuesday—Mars; Wednesday—Mercury; Thursday—Jupiter; Friday—Venus; Saturday—Saturn. Now each of these planets is, in turn, associated with a metal: Sun—gold; Moon—silver; Mars—iron; Mercury—mercury; Jupiter—tin; Venus—copper; Saturn—lead.

From the table of correspondences used in candle-burning magick, we know what specific properties

are governed by the days of the week, and can therefore correlate those properties with the metals:

Sunday: *Sun, gold*
  Fortune; hope; money

Monday: *Moon, silver*
  Merchandise; dreams; theft

Tuesday: *Mars, iron*
  Matrimony; war; enemies; prison

Wednesday: *Mercury, mercury*
  Debt; fear; loss

Thursday: *Jupiter, tin*
  Honor; riches; clothing; desires

Friday: *Venus, copper*
  Love; friendship; strangers

Saturday: *Saturn, lead*
  Life; building; doctrine; protection

So, for example, knowing that Friday is associated
with love (ruled by Venus) and that the metal is copper, we now know that a love talisman, for greatest effect, should be made of copper.

Mercury gives a bit of a problem in that it is a liquid metal. It could be used by containing it in a
miniature bottle, but it is more usual and a lot easier,
to substitute either gold, silver, or parchment. Today,
also, many substitute aluminum. Parchment, gold, or

silver can likewise be used in place of any of the other metals if they are unobtainable, but obviously the specified metal would be the best.

Having chosen your metal, what should you inscribe on it? There are many talismanic designs shown in occult books, taken from such old grimoires as *The Greater and Lesser Keys of Solomon, The Black Pullet, Le Dragon Rouge,* and similar. But just copying these designs, without knowing their meanings or significance, and without personalizing them, is completely useless. You need to work specifically for your problem. The most common form a talisman takes is a metal disc worn on a chain, as a pendant. On one side of the disc place the personalization and on the other side the objective. Let us do an example.

Jane Doe wants to get married. She already has a boyfriend, so love is not what she is seeking. Looking at the correspondences, we see that Mars rules matrimony. She needs a talisman to bring matrimony. The metal for Mars is iron. Jane can either obtain an iron disc and engrave on it, or she can opt for the easier gold, silver, or parchment.

She is going to personalize one side of it. She will do this by putting her name and date of birth on it. She can use one of the magickal alphabets for the name. She can also add her astrological Sun sign, Rising sign (ascendant) and Moon sign, plus ruling planets. These can all be arranged on the disc. There is no special pattern that has to be followed; anything

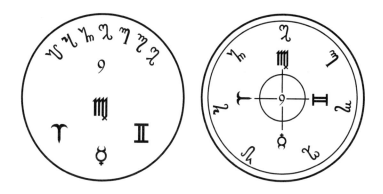

Figure 15
Sample Talisman

aesthetically pleasing will do. Figure 15 gives two possible alternatives. Each has the same symbols, but in different arrangement.

As each of the symbols is engraved, or drawn, Jane should concentrate on herself, seeing herself as she best likes herself—charming, happy, self-confident. On the reverse side of the talisman, she should put symbols traditionally associated with marriage: wedding bells, flowers, rings, hearts, etc. Or, she could place a sigil constructed from numerological squares, as follows.

From numerology (chapter 3) we know that the numerological value of the word *matrimony* is 4 + 1 + 2 + 9 + 9 + 4 + 6 + 5 + 7 = 47 = 11 = 2.

You now construct a magick square (more on magick squares, generally, below) containing all the numbers one through nine (fig. 16). Now, starting at the first letter (m, 4) draw a small circle, to indicate the start, and then draw a line to the second letter/number: a = 1. Follow on to 2 and then to 9. There are two nines in the word so stop-and-start there with small triangles (see illustration). Continue through to the last letter and draw another small circle to indicate the end.

At square 2, the numerological total (47 = 11 = 2), draw a large square. The finished figure will look like figure 17a. Transferred off the squares, it will look like figure 17b.

What you see in 17b, then, is the sigil for matrimony. Jane can inscribe this on the reverse of the talisman. As she does so, she should concentrate her thoughts on the marriage itself; see herself as a bride, see herself and her husband wearing wedding bands, see the ceremony taking place . . . such a sigil would be far more potent than the traditional bells, hearts, and rings, of course. Incidentally, the magickal square

4	9	2	15
3	5	7	15
8	1	6	15

15 + 15 + 15 = 45

45 = 4 + 5 = 9

Figure 16
The Square of Lo Shu
(Square of Saturn)

4	9	2
3	5	7
8	1	6

Figure 17a   *Figure 17b*

Making Magick Square Talisman

used is the ancient Chinese "Square of Lo Shu" and is the best for constructing sigils based on numerology.

The day associated with matrimony is Tuesday. That is the day Jane Doe should make her talisman. She should also choose a Tuesday that is in the waxing phase of the Moon. Whatever the purpose of the talisman, follow the same procedure. Find the day and the metal associated with your desire; personalize one side of the appropriate metal; take the key word and, from the magick square, find the appropriate sigil; inscribe the sigil on the reverse side, concentrating as necessary; finally, consecrate the talisman (again during the waxing of the Moon) by washing it in salt-water and holding it in the smoke of incense.

Now, for extra potency, use color on your talisman. One way is simply to always make your talisman on parchment and use colored inks for marking it. Use the color associated with the person's Sun sign for writing their name and personal symbols. On the reverse side, use the color associated with the day for marking the sigil:

Sunday: Yellow

Monday: White

Tuesday: Red

Wednesday: Purple

Thursday: Blue

Friday: Green

Saturday: Indigo (or black)

So, going back to Jane Doe's matrimony talisman, if she is a Virgo, then she would write her name and other personal data in violet and, on the reverse, draw her sigil in red (red for Tuesday, the day for matrimony). If you want to stick with metal talismans, of course, there is no reason why you should not paint the markings on, in the appropriate colors.

To finish off, instead of hanging the talisman on a chain around your neck, hang it on a double length of colored thread or silk—the two colors used in the marking.

Magick Squares

Magick squares are found in many parts of the world at different times. Basically, they are talismanic figures. The best known, and perhaps most varied collection is to be found in *The Book of Sacred Magic of Abramelin the Mage,* translated by S. L. MacGregor Mathers. The squares consist of letters arranged to form the square, though numbers can also be used. Probably the oldest example is found in China as "The Square of Lo Shu" (fig. 16). It consists of the numbers one through nine arranged in such a way that they add up to fifteen in all directions—horizontally, vertically, and diagonally. This particular square is also found in Qabalistic writings as the Square of Saturn (there are squares for each of seven planets).

Using color, and constructing them carefully, magick squares can be very potent talismans in themselves. Some of the more common ones are shown in figures 18 and 19.

Important rules to follow when writing in the symbols (numbers or letters):

1. The symbols should all be of the same size.

2. They must not touch the lines (which should be perfectly drawn).

3. You must not allow your shadow to cover the square as you work on it.

4. The symbols must be written in their sequence.

5. You must concentrate on the purpose of the talisman as you construct it.

6. Be absolutely confident of the success you will achieve.

For rule number three, work facing the Sun. This way, your shadow will not fall completely over the square, so long as you are careful. For rule number five, visualize the end product. For example, if working to cure a sore throat, see yourself shouting and singing. If working to get a job, see yourself in that job, working and happily employed.

Concentrate on what you are doing, as you work on the square, not allowing any interruption.

Before starting on the construction, it is a good idea to meditate on what you want. In making the square, first consider its purpose. Let us use the health square as an example. Suppose you want a talisman to wear or carry to retain good health. Here, blue would be a good, basic color. So, make the square on blue paper (a good quality, fairly thick paper is recommended). Red is the color of blood; also the color for health and strength. A good, vibrant, red ink, then, would be a good choice for the inscription. In red, draw the lines and write in the numbers or letters.

Make sure the lines are carefully drawn and that all the letters are of uniform size, not touching the lines. Draw them in, concentrating on your good health the whole time.

When using a square with letters rather than numbers, use one of the magickal alphabets. Example: the square to obtain the love of a woman, with the letters in Theban (fig. 20).

Remember that colors are important. They make the square far more potent than if it was just done on plain parchment with black ink.

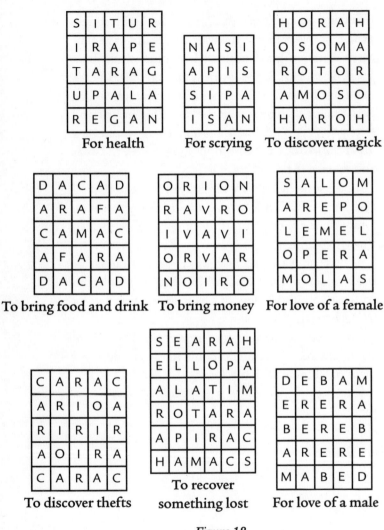

S	I	T	U	R
I	R	A	P	E
T	A	R	A	G
U	P	A	L	A
R	E	G	A	N

For health

N	A	S	I
A	P	I	S
S	I	P	A
I	S	A	N

For scrying

H	O	R	A	H
O	S	O	M	A
R	O	T	O	R
A	M	O	S	O
H	A	R	O	H

To discover magick

D	A	C	A	D
A	R	A	F	A
C	A	M	A	C
A	F	A	R	A
D	A	C	A	D

To bring food and drink

O	R	I	O	N
R	A	V	R	O
I	V	A	V	I
O	R	V	A	R
N	O	I	R	O

To bring money

S	A	L	O	M
A	R	E	P	O
L	E	M	E	L
O	P	E	R	A
M	O	L	A	S

For love of a female

C	A	R	A	C
A	R	I	O	A
R	I	R	I	R
A	O	I	R	A
C	A	R	A	C

To discover thefts

S	E	A	R	A	H
E	L	L	O	P	A
A	L	A	T	I	M
R	O	T	A	R	A
A	P	I	R	A	C
H	A	M	A	C	S

To recover
something lost

D	E	B	A	M
E	R	E	R	A
B	E	R	E	B
A	R	E	R	E
M	A	B	E	D

For love of a male

Figure 18
Other Magick Squares

4	14	15	1
9	7	6	12
5	11	10	8
16	2	3	13

Jupiter: success/blue

57	78	29	70	21	62	15	54	5
6	38	79	50	71	22	63	14	46
47	7	39	80	31	72	23	55	15
16	48	8	40	81	32	64	24	56
57	17	49	9	41	73	33	65	25
26	58	18	50	1	42	74	34	66
67	27	59	10	51	2	43	75	35
36	68	19	60	11	52	3	44	76
77	28	69	20	61	12	53	4	45

Moon: white

6	32	3	34	35	1
7	11	27	28	8	30
19	14	16	15	23	24
18	20	22	21	17	13
25	29	10	9	26	12
36	5	33	4	2	31

Sun: yellow

22	47	16	41	10	35	4
5	23	43	17	42	11	29
30	6	24	49	18	36	12
13	31	7	25	43	19	37
38	14	32	1	26	44	20
21	39	8	33	2	27	45
16	15	40	9	34	3	38

Venus: green

8	58	59	5	4	62	63	1
49	15	14	52	53	11	10	56
41	23	22	44	45	19	18	48
32	34	35	29	28	38	39	25
40	26	27	37	36	30	31	33
17	47	46	20	21	43	42	24
9	55	54	12	13	51	50	16
64	2	3	61	60	6	7	57

Mercury: purple

Figure 19
Other Magick Squares

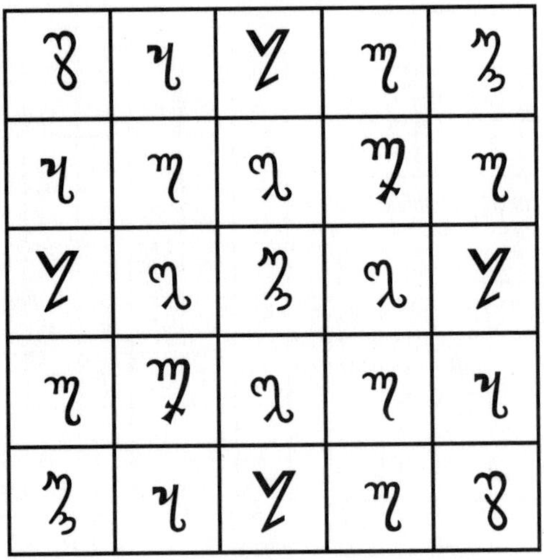

Figure 20
Square Using Magical Alphabet

6

Color in Healing

In this and the following chapter, I will deal with the use of color in healing. I must make a point of saying that the information given is the result of my own personal research into the history of this use and it in no way reflects any engagement, on my part, in rendering professional medical advice. Such advice should be sought from a competent professional person.

In this present chapter, I will explain the use of color in such techniques as color projection, color breathing, and auric healing. Later, in chapter 7, I will detail

hydrochromopathy,   gem therapy, graphochromopathy,and therapy through music and sound.

Color Projection

The most effective way to use color for healing, in
fact, altogether the most effective form of chromotherapy, is *chromopathy*—color projection. This has
been known for centuries. The ancient Egyptians
and, before them, the Atlanteans, used it, though it
then fell into disuse until it was rediscovered at the
beginning of the 20th century. In recent years it has
grown into a rapidly developing serious study, recognized and used especially in Europe and the Far East.

As I mentioned in the introduction to this book,
our bodies select from sunlight whatever colors they
need for balance. But we can boost this process by
first determining what color(s) we are lacking and
then give ourselves a concentrated *shot* to supplement
the sunlight.

The best way to get the different colors is by projecting light through filters, or gels—the colored
sheets of gelatine and cellulose acetate used in the-
atrical lighting. I use a product called Roscolene, put
out by the Adams Lighting Company (33 Bristol St.,
Cambridge, MA 02141). It is available in a wide variety of colors (approximately eighty), though you can
start with the seven basics. It comes in sheets 20"x
24". Some researchers have found the use of colored

silk placed in frames work well. Dr. George White suggests that a good grade manufactured under the trade name Faile-Matines is suitable. Whatever you use, the idea is to project the suitably colored light onto the body of the patient for a certain period of time, allowing the body (or specific part of the body) to absorb it.

The simplest way to use the color sheets is to cover a window with the appropriate color* and then sit in the light of it. The only problem here is that you need a sunny day for it to work well, and, for best results, there should only be one window in the room and it-should be completely covered with the color (if more than one window, then all should be completely covered with the color).

Equally effective, yet far more adaptable, is the use of a projector of some sort, in lieu of sun through a window. The projector can be set up anywhere and focused either on the entire body or just on a specific part. The light source, you see, does not have to be the Sun . . . artificial light will work as well, though incandescent is preferable to fluorescent.

You can fasten a sheet of colored gel over a regular lamp—a gooseneck desk lamp is good—and use that. Or you can use a photographic slide projector. Buy a box of blank slide frames (usually cardboard or plastic), as used for mounting 35mm color transparencies, and fit a rectangle of colored gel in each.

---

*I'll be detailing what colors to use for what, later in the chapter.

You can then use them in the projector and focus either on the body as a whole or on one particular section. I use a Kodak carousel projector.

For working on small areas, I use a number of Gaf Viewmaster projectors (model 300M). You may remember Viewmaster from your younger days, when you would drop a cardboard disc into the binocular-style viewer and look into it to see pictures in three dimensions. Well, in addition to the hand-held viewers, the Gaf company produces small projectors for their series of discs. These projectors do not give a stereo effect, however, simply projecting a single one of each of the two coupled transparencies on the disc. What I did was to carefully remove the phototransparencies from a disc—one from each of the pairs was all that was necessary (fig. 21)—and replace them with colored gels. I then had one disc with seven of my working colors on it.

Properties of Colors

For a complete listing of which color can be used for what, it would take a complete book in itself. Dinshah P. Ghadiali, a pioneer in chromopathy, gives the following general breakdown in his excellent work *Spectro-chrome Home Guide* (Malaga, N. J., 1933). I consider it one of the best (where numbered areas of the body are mentioned, refer to figure 22).

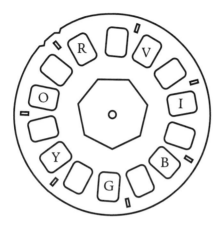

Figure 21
Color Projection Disk

Red

Sensory stimulant: An agent that increases the activity of the sensory nervous system, energizing the senses of vision, smell, taste, hearing, and touch.

Liver energizer: An agent that activates the liver. Use on Area 7.

Irritant: An agent that irritates.

Vescicant: An agent that blisters.

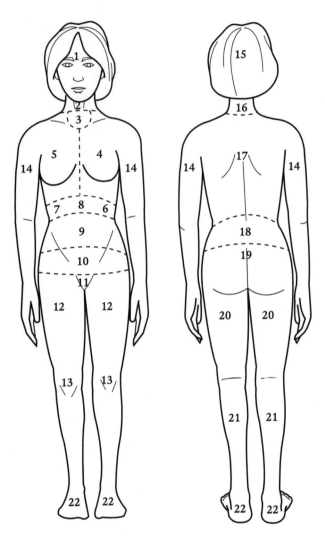

Figure 22
Color Stimulating Areas

Pustulant: An agent that suppurates.

Rubefacient: An agent that reddens the skin.

Caustic: An agent that burns and corrodes.

Hemoglobin builder: An agent that builds the coloring matter of the red blood corpuscles, in the liver. Area 7.

Orange

Respiratory stimulant: An agent that increases breathing. Areas 4, 5, and 17.

Parathyroid depressant: An agent that diminishes the functional activity of the four parathyroid glands, embedded in the right and left thyroid glands. Area 3.

Thyroid energizer: An agent that increases the functional activity of the thyroid glands. Area 3.

Antispasmodic: An agent that relieves spasm or sudden, violent, involuntary, rigid contraction due to muscular action.

Galactagogue: An agent that increases the secretion of milk after childbirth, by stimulating the mammary glands. Areas 4 and 5.

Antirachitic: An agent that corrects rickets or bone softness.

Emetic: An agent that induces orelim (oral elimination) or vomiting, by irritating. Area 8.

Carminative: An agent that relieves flatulence or distension of the stomach or intestines with gases. Areas 8 and 9.

Stomachic: An agent that tones the stomach. Area 8.

Aromatic: An agent that induces the qualities of spices. A stimulant.

Lung builder: An agent that builds the lungs. Areas 4, 5, and 17.

Yellow

Motor stimulant: An agent that increases the functional activity of the motor nervous system, which energizes the muscles into motion.

Alimentary tract energizer: An agent that activates the food passages. Areas 8, 9, 10, 18, and 19.

Lymphatic activator: An agent that increases the functional activity of the lymphatic glands for nutrition.

Splenic depressant: An agent that decreases the functional activity of the spleen. Area 6.

Digestant: An agent that aids the process of converting food into materials fit to be absorbed and assimilated in the physical body, by stimulating the gastric and intestinal glands and pancreas. Areas 8, 9, and 18.

Cathartic: An agent that produces increase in back-elim (back elimination) or quickens purgation. Areas 9, 10, 18, and 19.

Cholagogue: An agent that accelerates the flow of bile. Area 7.

Anthelmintic: An agent that is destructive to most worms.

Nerve builder: An agent that builds the nerves by stimulating the choroid gland for cerebrospinal fluid secretion. Area 15.

Lemon

Cerebral stimulant: An agent that increases the functional activity of the brain. Areas 1 and 15.

Thymus activator: An agent that increases the action of the thymus gland. Areas 4 and 5.

Antacid: An agent that neutralizes or counteracts acidity.

Chronic alterative: An agent that produces a favorable change in the processes of nutrition and repair in persistent disorders.

Antiscorbutic: An agent that corrects scurvy, a disorder of nutrition and dietetic errors.

Laxative: An agent that mildly loosens the intestines. Areas 9, 10, 18, and 19.

Expectorant: An agent that promotes ejection by spitting of mucus or other fluids from the lungs and windpipe. Areas 2, 4, 5, and 17.

Bone builder: An agent that builds the body skeleton.

Green

Pituitary stimulant: An agent that increases the functional activity of the pituitary gland in the head. Area 1.

Disinfectant: An agent that destroys rotting materials.

Purificatory: An agent that purifies.

Antiseptic: An agent that prevents decay.

Germicide: An agent that kills germs.

Bactericide: An agent that destroys microorganisms or bacteria.

Detergent: An agent that cleans.

Muscle and tissue builder: An agent that builds muscles and tissues.

Turquoise

Cerebral depressant: An agent that decreases the functional activity of the brain. Areas 1 and 15.

Acute alterative: An agent that produces a favorable change in the processes of nutrition and repair, in recent disorders.

Acid: An agent that neutralizes or counteracts an alkali.

Tonic: An agent that tones the general system.

Skin builder: An agent that builds the skin.

Blue

Antipruritic: An agent that prevents or relieves itching.

Diaphoretic: An agent that encourages perspiration.

Febrifuge: An agent that dispels or reduces fever.

Counterirritant: An agent that allays irritation.

Anodyne: An agent that soothes suffering.

Demulcent: An agent that allays the irritation of abraded or scratched surfaces.

Vitality builder: An agent that builds the life principle by stimulating the pineal gland. Area 1.

Indigo

Parathyroid stimulant: An agent that increases the functional activity of the four parathyroid glands embedded in the right and left thyroid glands. Area 3.

Thyroid depressant: An agent that decreases the functional activity of the thyroid glands. Area 3.

Respiratory depressant: An agent that decreases breathing. Areas 4, 5, and 17.

Astringent: An agent that causes contraction and arrests discharges.

Sedative: An agent that allays activity and excitement.

Pain reliever: An agent that allays suffering.

Hemostatic: An agent that checks the flow of blood.

Inspissator: An agent that dries or thickens.

Phagocyte builder: An agent that builds cells that destroy harmful microorganisms.

Violet

Splenic stimulant: An agent that increases the functional activity of the spleen. Area 8.

Cardiac depressant: An agent that decreases the functional activity of the heart. Area 4.

Lymphatic depressant: An agent that decreases the functional activity of the lymphatic glands for nutrition.

Motor depressant: An agent that decreases the functional activity of the motor nervous system, which energizes the muscles into motion.

Leucocyte builder: An agent that builds the white corpuscles in the spleen. Area 6.

Purple

Venous stimulant: An agent that increases the functional activity of the veins.

Renal depressant: An agent that decreases the functional activity of the kidneys. Area 18.

Antimalarial: An agent that prevents or removes malaria.

Vasodilator: An agent that causes expansion of the blood vessels, lowering the blood pressure.

Anaphrodisiac: An agent that decreases sexual desires.

Narcotic: An agent that produces stupor.

Hypnotic: An agent that induces sleep.

Antipyretic: An agent that lowers body temperature.

Analgesic: An agent that decreases sensitivity to pain.

Magenta

Suprarenal stimulant: An agent that increases the functional activity of the adrenal glands on the kidneys. Area 18.

Cardiac energizer: An agent that increases the functional activity of the heart. Area 4.

Diuretic: An agent that increases or promotes the secretion of frontelim (front elimination).

Emotional equilibrator: An agent that stabilizes the emotions.

Auric builder: An agent that builds the aura or the radio-emanations of the chemical body.

Scarlet

Arterial stimulant: An agent that increases the functional activity of the arteries.

Renal energizer: An agent that increases the functional activity of the kidneys. Area 18.

Genital excitant: An agent that stirs the functional activity of the genital organs. Area 11.

Aphrodisiac: An agent that arouses the sexual desires. Area 11.

Emmenagogue: An agent that stimulates the ovelim (ovarian elimination) or menstruation.

Vasoconstrictor: An agent that causes contraction of the blood vessels, raising blood pressure.

Ecbolic: An agent that causes or accelerates expulsion of a fetus.

Length of Treatment

Project the color for at least thirty minutes each day. I find that most practitioners treat for one thirty-minute period in the morning, and then a second thirty-minute period in the evening.

Days to Treat

An essential part of life is rhythm. Undoubtedly a woman's menstrual cycle is one of the best recognized rhythms. It is (on average) a twenty-eight-day cycle. Many women find a change in their moods within a week or ten days before the onset of their period, so there is nothing new to the observation of a twenty-eight-day periodicity to emotions. And I am sure everyone has noticed that they have *good* days and *bad* days.

Around the turn of the century (1895–1902) Herman Swaboda, professor of psychology at the University of Vienna, became interested in the rhythmic cycles of humans and detailed a twenty-three-day cycle in certain aspects of illness. He considered this a masculine rhythm, in contradistinction to the woman's twenty-eight-day rhythm. He was, however, very much aware of the bisexuality of humans—each having component parts of the opposite sex in their makeup. Some years later, in the 1920s, Alfred Telscher, an engineering instructor, noted that his students' high and low peaks had a thirty-one-day periodicity.

April

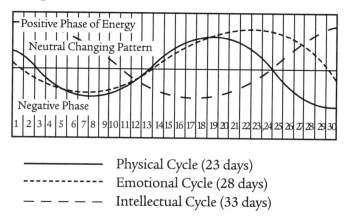

—————————— Physical Cycle (23 days)
------------------ Emotional Cycle (28 days)
— — — — — Intellectual Cycle (33 days)

Figure 23
Biorhythms Chart

There are, then, three basic human rhythms. They are referred to as biorhythms: a physical twenty-three-day cycle; an emotional twenty-eight-day cycle; and an intellectual thirty-three-day cycle.

For over twenty years, physicians and psychologists observed and charted these changes. They observed that these patterns covered these three main aspects and that each rhythm never varied. Thus, it was possible to forecast good days and bad days; high energy days and low energy days. And, most importantly, the *critical* days . . . the days when most accidents occur, when you are most likely to make poor decisions, and when you are most vulnerable to illness. These are days when the physical and emotional curves pass closely together from the positive phase of the graph into the negative phase (fig. 23). As professionals in Europe took up and furthered this study, it was observed that, by taking advantage of these circadian rhythms, surgeons could cut down on postoperative complications and, for example, on their critical days, airlines and bus lines could keep pilots and drivers off duty.

You can use these rhythms in the healing process, for an individual's personal biorhythm can be more important than the phases of the Moon. For example, if you are working to aid in the mending of someone's broken limb, working in the waxing phase of the Moon would be good, but working when the person's individual physical biorhythm was on the increase would be much better.

How do you find the individual's cycles? You can obtain tables to help you compute the rhythms, and instruments (such as *Biomatre*) to do it for you. Mathematically, you need to add up the total number of days in an individual's life, from the date of birth to the first day of the particular month for which the chart is to be constructed. This total is then divided by 23, 28, and 33, respectively. These divisions indicate how many times each cycle has run a complete span. The remainders show the position of each rhythm on the first day of the month being studied. It is obviously far easier to use a set of tables or a calculator, so I will not pursue the calculations here. On the subject of biorhythms, I particularly recommend George S. Thommen's book, *Is This Your Day?* (Crown, N. Y., 1973).

When working with chromopathy, then, it is good to have a copy of the patient's biorhythm and to plan the color treatments so that they take place when his/her physical cycle is on the increase (if you are working on a mental problem, then when the emotional cycle is on the increase).

Diet

Along with the projection of color should go careful attention to diet, and even here you can be guided by color. For example, when the subject requires red, it is a good idea to incorporate into one's diet such items as beetroot, red cabbage, radishes, red currants, red plums, etc.

For **red:** Beetroot, red cabbage, radishes, red currants, red plums.

For **orange:** Carrots, pumpkins, rutabagas, oranges, apricots, tangerines, peaches.

For **yellow:** Golden corn, parsnips, yams, sweet potatoes, honeydew melons, pineapples, bananas, lemons, grapefruit.

For **green:** Green vegetables and fruits that are not too alkaline or acid in their chemical reaction.

For **blue:** Blueberries, damsons, plums, bilberries.

For **indigo:** As for blue and for violet, alternating.

For **violet:** Purple broccoli, beets, grapes, blackberries.

Color Breathing

This is something that can be done at the same time as color projection, yet, if necessary, can also be done quite separately, at any time and in any place.

When working with projected colored light, it is advantageous to visualize the very air itself as being colored and hence, to breathe in that colored air. Working with, for example, a blue light, the subject breathes deeply and *absorbs* the blue into his or her body. The person feels it filling the lungs and permeating throughout the entire body, reinforcing the action of the light on the outer surface. A suggested regimen, at that time, is the breathing exercise detailed in chapter 1, pages 10–12, but very consciously and deliberately breathing in *colored air* throughout the exercise.

For a general tonic and rejuvenator, it is a good idea, at least once a week, to breathe in the seven main colors in turn, and use them to cleanse the chakra centers. It can be done as part of one of your regular meditation periods. Here is the best way to do it.

Sit as previously described, in chapter 1, but when you come to directing the cone of color to each specific chakra (fig. 3), go a little further than that. Direct the color through the cone (let us use the green as an example), and also breathe it in through the nose and send it down to the thymus, to the heart area. But not only see/feel it absorbed into that area, see and feel it swirling around, very fast, in a clockwise direction. Keep it swirling and spinning, as fast as you can, for at least one full minute, then let it slow and stop. Pass on, then, to the thyroid and do the same thing with blue; breathing it in and directing it through the cone. Swirl it around the throat chakra rapidly for a full minute, then slow and move to the pineal (I used green as an example, to start, but you would normally start with the perineum red, of course, and continue through all seven).

One of the joys of color breathing is that it can be done any time and anywhere, with no equipment. For example, suppose you have a touch of rheumatism in your left hand. While you are sitting watching television (or while you are driving to work, or anywhere or time), you can breathe deeply and see/believe/know that you are breathing in blue air. Breathe deeply and direct that blue air through your body to your left hand.

If you have difficulty visualizing a stream of blue air coming into you, then think first of yourself being completely surrounded and enclosed in a ball of blue light. Everything about you is blue. Then, as you breathe, you cannot help but breathe in blue air. Now as you breathe and direct it to your hand, breathe in deeply and hold the breath for as long as you can. As you are holding it, see, in your mind's eye, the hand loose and free and completely without the rheumatism.

This is a very important part of color breathing for health. In addition to breathing in the appropriate color, hold your breath for as long as you can and visualize the end product. See the cure affected. If you are breathing cobalt blue for laryngitis, see yourself shouting and singing; if you are breathing red for asthma, see yourself breathing deeply and freely and unrestrictedly; if you are breathing green for a broken leg, see yourself running and jumping; if you are breathing yellow for constipation. . . . Well, you get the idea!

A lady named Yvonne Martine, of Indiana, came up with the idea of breathing pink and directing it to her face to erase wrinkles and maintain her beauty. Needless to say, it worked. Many people have since tried it with amazing results. When I first heard of it, I decided to experiment myself. Whilst driving to and from work each day, I would spend ten minutes breathing pink and directing it to my face. I kept this up for a year. Today I am invariably taken to be anywhere from ten to fifteen years younger than my actual age!

If should be needless to say that with color breathing, results are not instantaneous. Indeed, it can take a very long time for it to have effect, though it will have effect. Color breathing is best used as a supplement to direct light chromology, or to the other therapeutic uses of color detailed in this and the next chapter.

Auric Healing

The body is actually composed of seven distinct elements. The first three (solid, liquid, and gas) form the physical body. The fourth element is called the etheric body and interpenetrates the physical. Generally, the etheric body extends beyond the confines of the physical body by about an inch. Next is the astral body. It extends several inches beyond the etheric body. Then, beyond the astral body, are the mental and spiritual bodies. Due to their elasticity, and the speed at which they function, it is impossible to define physical limits to these last two (fig. 24).

Although the vibrations of the nonphysical bodies are too high a rate to be detected by the physical eye, the energy patterns that emanate can be seen by the adept. These energy patterns are what is known as the *aura*.

Usually the energy of the etheric body is detected, or *seen* first, because of its denseness. As your perceptions improve, you can begin to detect the energy that

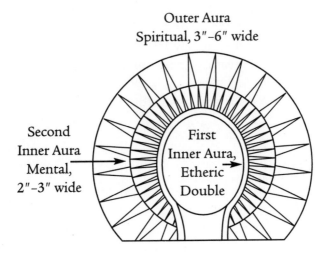

Outer Aura
Spiritual, 3"–6" wide

Second
Inner Aura
Mental,
2"–3" wide

First
Inner Aura,
Etheric
Double

Figure 24
Auras

radiates beyond the etheric body. Often it can be seen flowing, ebbing, and spiraling, much like the northern lights. The colors detected are usually indicative of the person's state of being. Thus, a person with a deeply spiritual state may exhibit blue and lavender. A person deeply in love may show pink, etc. You should be cautioned about trying to see what another person sees, however. If you and a friend are reading auras, do not be surprised if one of you detects blue and the other detects yellow. Neither of you is necessarily wrong. Individual sensitivities are different and you are more sensitive to certain vibrations while your friend is more receptive to others.

Any state of the individual's being causes reactions in the aura. Emotional states will primarily affect the color. Physical conditions not only affect color but also cause peculiarities in the patterns of the aura, such as vortexes, holes, and sometimes dark spots. You should be careful in your treatment of information concerning auras. You may think that someone has a physical problem because of what seems to be a defect in his or her aura. Ask the person if he or she has a problem in that particular area. But, if the person denies it, drop the issue. What may appear serious to you at the time, could be just a minor irritation that is nearly healed. Remember, the power of suggestion is strong and could turn out to be very damaging to some people.

The aura is sometimes referred to as "the odic force." In Christian art, from the fifth to the sixteenth centuries, it was often depicted around the heads of people believed to possess great spiritual power. There it was referred to as *halos* or *glorias*. Around the heads, in paintings of Moslem prophets, it appears as a ring of flames. Crowns and priests' headdresses symbolize the aura (fig. 25). In sculpture, Michaelangelo's statue of Moses depicts him with horns . . . which mystifies many. The reason is that in translation the word for *horns* was confused with the similar word for *rays* (of light).

In 1858, Baron Karl von Reichenbach, an industrial chemist, claimed to have discovered certain radiations coming from magnets, crystals, plants, and animals,

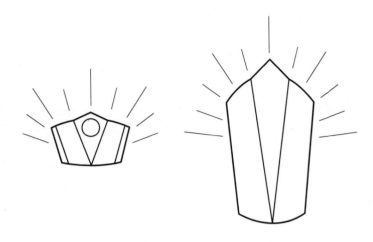

Figure 25
Auras Symbolized as Crowns

which could be seen and felt by certain people (sensitives). In 1911, Dr. Walter Kilner, of St. Thomas' Hospital, London, devised ways of showing these radiations. One way was by looking through a dilute solution of a dye called *dicyanin* (a product of coal tar), and the other was by first looking at a bright light through a strong alcoholic solution, then looking at the subject. This last method, however, proved to be very dangerous, causing damage to the eyes. Kilner did perfect his dicyanin method and produced what is known as the *Kilner Screen*.

But the aura is best seen without artificial aid. Have your subject stand against a dark background and look, directing your gaze at the position of the subject's third eye (between, and a little above, the eyebrows). You may find it helpful to squint slightly at first. You will become aware of the aura around his or her head though, at first, when you try to move your gaze to look directly at it . . . it will disappear! Do not worry. You will eventually be able to study it directly but, to start with, just keep your focus on that third eye and look at the aura peripherally. If you have no success with the subject against a dark background, then try a light background; some have success with one, some with the other.

The aura will be most obvious around the head, unless the body is naked, in which case it will be seen clearly all around. The entire aura is called the *aureole;* the head aura is the *nimbus.* You may notice that to the person's left there is generally an orange color, and to their right a bluish color. If you move your hands toward the body you will feel warmth on their left and coolness on their right. Interestingly, a bar magnet gives corresponding sensations. With the north end cool and blue, and the south warm and orange (fig. 26), the aura can be felt. If you stand in front of your subject, with your hands extended on either side of his or her head, and the palms in toward him or her, you can feel it. Gradually, move your hands in toward the head. As you approach (perhaps about four to six inches away) you will feel a tingling sensation, or a warmth, or a feeling of pressure building up. Move your hands in and out and get that sensation.

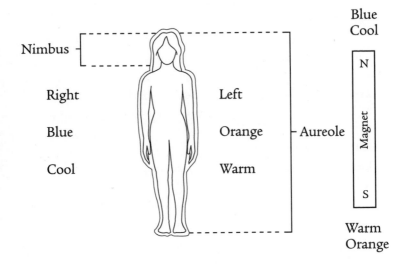

Figure 26
Color and Feel of Aureole

Auric healing is when the condition of a person is changed by the healer visualizing him or her surrounded by a specific color light.

For the nervous system, the auric colors used in mental concentration are: violet and lavender for relaxing, soothing effects; grass green for invigorating effects; and yellows and orange for inspiring effects.

For the blood and organs of the body, clear dark blues are soothing; grass greens are invigorating; and bright reds are stimulating.

For cases of fever, high blood pressure, or hysteria, think of blue.

For cases of chill, or lack of bodily warmth, think of red.

So, for example, if a person is complaining of feeling hot, has a fever, and is sweating profusely, you can help immeasurably by concentrating on seeing him or her completely surrounded by, and absorbed in, a blue light. If he or she has a stomach pain, then direct a soothing light-green color to that area. For someone with a nervous headache, see his or her head surrounded by violet or lavender light. Keep this up for as long as you can. For a bleeding, direct clear dark blue light to the cut.

In each case, keep up these visualizations for as long as you can. Then, finish them off with a pure, white light projection. One of the advantages of auric healing is that it can be done without the subject's knowledge. The subject may not believe in it; may not want your help; may not understand what you want to do. But also he or she will not know when you are mentally projecting healing auric color waves at him or her.

7
Advanced Color Healing

*O*ne of the exciting things about chromotherapy is that it can be used in so many different ways. In the last chapter, I spoke of color projection, color breathing, and auric healing. Now I will look at healing with color-charged water, distant or absent healing through photographs, the healing properties of precious and semiprecious stones, and the healing power of sound.

Hydrochromopathy

Many psychic healers will take a glass of water and, cupping it in their hands, *charge* it with their healing powers. It is then given to the patient to drink. This practice can be expanded by charging water with color; something anyone can do.

Through visiting antique stores, flea markets, garage sales, swap meets, etc., it is possible to obtain a collection of glass bottles, each in one of the seven main colors. The colors should be as *true* as possible (see Introduction regarding wavelengths). If you cannot get colored bottles or until such time as you can, use a clear glass bottle and fasten a colored gel around it (fig. 27).

The bottle is filled with water and placed in the window to absorb the light rays through its color (be it glass or gel). The water should preferably be pure spring water. Failing that, distilled water will do. Again, projected artificial light will do in place of sunlight, but it is certainly easy enough to simply stand the bottle in the window since there is no need for direct sunlight to shine on it . . . it can sit there on a cloudy day and still absorb. It should be in the window for at least an hour (three hours on a cloudy day) before using, and actually can be left there all day.

Feeling *down*, sluggish, no energy? Charge the bottle with red and then drink a wineglassful of it three times a day. You will be surprised how the red-charged water will pick you up. It is a great tonic.

Hot and feverish? How about drinking some blue-charged water; again, a wine-glassful three times a day. Green-charged water is a very good general tonic.

Be guided by the same principles used in color projection. In fact, it is a good idea to supplement your chromopathy (color projection) treatment with the hydrochromopathy (color-charged water). One of the joys of hydrochromopathy is that it is so cheap . . . and it does not call for a prescription!

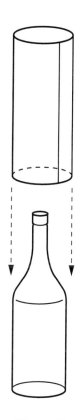

Figure 27
**Bottle for
Hydrochromopathy**

Graphochromopathy

One of the oldest forms of magick is that termed sympathetic magick. To quote from my book *Witchcraft from the Inside* (Llewellyn Publications, St. Paul, Minn., 1975):

> Similar things, it was held (in Palaeolithic times) have similar effects; like influences like. Magick was used to direct the hunt. One man would represent the god and supervise the magic. . . . A model of the animal to be hunted was made, in clay, on the floor of the cave and, under the priest's direction, was attacked by the men of the tribe. Successful in "killing" the clay animal the men could then go about the real thing confident that the hunt would go exactly as acted before the God.
>
> Evidence of this early religio-magick has been found in such places as the Caverne des Trois Fréres at Ariége, France. Here can be seen the cave-painting known as *The Sorcerer*. This shows a man dressed in the skin of a stag and wearing a mask and horns. In Dordogne is found another such figure wearing the horns of a bull, and playing some form of musical instrument. At le Tuc d'Audubert, Ariége, is a very realistic clay model of a bison. It is pock-marked with holes where it was literally attacked with spears and javelins. There is also a similarly holed model of a bear. The bear has been modelled without a head, but possesses a hole in the neck that originally held a stake from which was hung a real bear's head. On a

reindeer horn found at Laugerie Basse there is carved a prostrate man creeping up, on all fours, toward a grazing bison.

These actions, paintings and carvings, show how acting on a *representation* of a thing can actually affect the *real* thing. Taking it a step further, to a more modern example—albeit looking at a negative magick example, a Black Magician might take a photograph of his or her intended victim and stick it with pins, thus inflicting severe pain on the actual victim.

If the photograph can be used for evil ends, then it can just as easily be used for good purposes. By projecting color onto a photograph, we can sympathetically project that color on to the person shown in the photograph, and thus can promote healing in that person.

The first thing needed, of course, is a good clear photograph of the patient. He, or she, should be the only one in the photograph and the area to be healed should be both plainly visible and not covered by clothing. Obviously, the larger and clearer the photograph, the better. You can fasten the picture to a wall and use your projector to direct color on to it if you wish. Much easier, however, is to simply lay a sheet of the appropriately colored gel over the picture and stand it in the window. You can cut the gel to size and put it in a frame with the photo, if you prefer.

Once again, rather than sunlight you can use artificial light. Bill Finch, of St. Louis, Montana, designed a clear *chromo-light* unit, with a holder for the photograph and filter, and a low-watt bulb as the light source. It has reflective material on the inside top and sides. Incorporating a time switch, you could set up one of these units to switch on and off regularly (as I have done) and give constant treatments to the patient via his or her photograph.

One advantage of graphochromopathy is that you can effect healing when the patient is not present, and even when the patient is at a very great distance. It will take much longer to have effect than direct treatment, of course, but over a period of time it can be very beneficial. It is recommended to expose the photograph to the light for periods of at least an hour each, three times a day. The colors you use, of course, are the same as those you use for direct color projection.

Gem Therapy

The simplest way to use precious and semiprecious stones is to be guided by their colors. You have a sore throat? Wear a necklace of sapphires (or blue semiprecious stones). Asthma? Wear a pendant of orange sardonyx, or of amber, next to the skin. Rheumatism or arthritis in the hand? Rings of orange sardonyx or amber and blue sapphires on the fingers will help. Heartburn? Use a pendant of yellow opal.

Here is a list of gems and stones together with their colors and properties.

Agate: A banded, or irregular variegated, *chalcedony,* or crystalline quartz. Basically browns. Supposed to be good for the vision and also for hardening gums.

Amber: Fossilized resin, known variously as *burmite, pimetite, puccinite,* and *ruminite.* Good for throat problems, asthma, catarrh, also for aiding kidneys and liver.

Amethyst—*quartz:* Its color may be due to traces of manganese; can be anything from bluish-violet to deep purple in color. Traditionally sobers the drunk, but also good for expelling all types of poison and generally toning the body.

Beryl: Can appear white, yellow, green, or blue. Good for liver complaints.

Bloodstone (or *heliotrope*): Plasma variety of quartz. It contains small spots of red jasper, though it is basically green (from bright green to dark leaf green). Excellent for stopping bleeding and hemorrhages. Perfect for nosebleeds.

Carnelian—*chalcedony,* **or** *quartz:* Properties similar to bloodstone. A blood purifier.

Chrysolite (or *peridot)*—*olivine:* Usually olive green but sometimes yellow, brown, or even red. The greens and yellows will prevent fevers. Also said to prevent nightmares.

Coral—*calcium carbonate* **(skeletons of marine organisms):** Both red and white coral prevent bleeding. Also said to avert the "evil eye." Frequently hung about the necks of children for general good health. Good for scars and ulcers.

Crystal: A colorless quartz, or rock crystal. A symbol of purity and great spiritual protector.

Diamond: Considered something of a panacea, diamonds are especially good for coughs and mucus problems.

Emerald: Green variety of *beryl.* An antidote for poisons and very good for any diseases of the eyes.

Garnet: A deep red, good for the heart and as a general stimulant.

Jade: The green is a soothing, healing color. It is good for eye problems, kidney and urinary problems, and helps strengthen muscles.

Lapis lazuli—*lazurite:* Ranges in color from rich azure-blue through violet-blue to greenish-blue.

Good for eye problems. Very strong; should be used for short periods only.

Lapis linguis—*azurite;* various shades of blue. Good for meditating, and for bringing out your psychic abilities.

Lapis lingurius—*malachite:* Bright green. A protection from the "evil eye." Also good for rheumatism and cholera.

Moonstone—*adularia* **variety of** *orthoclase:* Pearly opalescent, similar to an opal. As the Moon rules the water, so does the moonstone govern affectations of a watery nature.

Opal: A noncrystalline form of quartz; a silica gem containing varying amounts of water. There is what is termed *precious* opal, *fire* opal, and *black* opal. The precious opal contains a wide variety of delicate colorings; blue, green, yellow, and pink being especially noticeable. Fire opal, as its name suggests, is predominantly red though it can vary to honey-yellow with glimpses of red. Black opal has a dark green background with black flecks. Pliny described the opal as "made up of the glories of the most precious gems . . . amongst them is the gentler fire of the ruby, the rich purple of the amethyst, the sea green of the emerald, glittering together in union indescribable." Opals are especially good for use on children, perhaps because of their delicate colors. The opal has been called "the gem of the gods," and is a stone of love . . . unless the lover be false, then beware! It is often used for mental illness.

Pearl: A concretion formed by a mollusk. The Hindus listed the pearl as one of the five precious stones in Vishnu's magickal necklace (the other four were diamond, emerald, ruby, and sapphire). It has always been considered a cure for irritability. It is an ideal jewel to use in conjunction with another colored stone; the pearl adding its soothing qualities to the other's healing.

Ruby—*corundum:* A deep red in color, the ruby is especially connected with the blood and with the red end of the spectrum. Good for chills and lack of body warmth, poor circulation, constipation, ulcers, boils, and biliousness.

Sardonyx—*cryptocrystalline quartz:* Different colored layers, mainly clear to brownish red along with white, brown, and black. Good for hemorrhages but mainly used for emotional states.

Topaz—*an alumino-fluorosilicate:* a mineral of granites and other igneous rocks. Usually brown, yellow, or pink (there is also a *false topaz* that is a brownish quartz). Used for soothing and calming, especially good for banishing nightmares and curing insomnia.

Turquoise—*copper-and-aluminum phosphate:* Light to dark blue, blue-green and green in color. For general healing. Good for lowering fevers and for calming nerves.

In her book *Healing and Regeneration Through Color* (New Age Press, Calif., 1976), Corinne Heline gives the following tables of correlation for metals and precious stones with days of the week and astrological signs.

Sunday: Gold and yellow gems

Monday: Pearls and all white stones

Tuesday: Rubies and all red stones

Wednesday: Turquoise, sapphire, and blue stones

Thursday: Amethyst and purple stones

Friday: Emerald and green stones

Saturday: Diamond; also black stones

Sign	Jewel	Metal	Color
Aries	Ruby, bloodstone, red jasper	Iron	Red
Taurus	Golden topaz, coral, emerald	Copper	Yellow
Gemini	Crystal, carbuncle, aquamarine	Mercury	Violet
Cancer	Emerald, moonstone	Silver	Green
Leo	Ruby, sardonyx, amber	Gold	Orange
Virgo	Pink jasper, turquoise, zircon	Mercury	Violet
Libra	Opal, diamond	Copper	Yellow
Scorpio	Agate, garnet, topaz	Iron	Red
Sagittarius	Amethyst	Tin	Purple
Capricorn:	Black-and-white onyx, beryl, jet	Lead	Blue

Sign	Jewel	Metal	Color
Aquarius:	Blue, sapphire	Lead	Indigo
Pisces:	Diamond, jade	Tin	Indigo

Music and Sound

In the case of a tuning fork vibrating in the air, the air is alternately compressed and rarefied by the action of the prongs, and the waves that are sent out consist of a series of alternate compressions and rarefactions. The number of vibrations made in one second by such a sounding body is called the *frequency*. The human ear can perceive sounds only within certain limits of frequency: as low as 30 decibels and as high as 24,000 decibels.

Color is to light what pitch is to sound. Color depends on the number of waves that strike the eye per second; pitch depends on the number of waves striking the ear per second. In color we have seven main colors. In music there are seven notes on the diatonic scale. The two have been equated, showing that every note gives off a color:

Middle	C	—	Red
	D	—	Orange
	E	—	Yellow
	F	—	Green
	G	—	Blue
	A	—	Indigo
	B	—	Violet

Just as you can supplement chromopathy with hydrochromopathy, so you can also further (or alternatively) supplement it with audiochromopathy. Have sound/music to accompany your light treatments. For example, if you are projecting yellow light on to the stomach area, for constipation, then throughout the treatment a repeated sounding of the note E (yellow), or the playing of music that has the E especially predominant, can be highly beneficial.

When working with the chakras (chapter 5), it can be very useful to tie-in the sound of the specific note with each chakra color. One way, of course, would be by chanting on that note.

The constant repetition of one note can become wearisome, if not quite aggravating, however. It is, therefore, worth looking a little deeper into the audio side of chromopathy.

Taking the semitones into consideration (sharps and flats) we actually have twelve notes ... the twelve semitones of the chromatic scale. These have been tied in to the astrological Sun signs to give *keynotes* for each sign:

Aries:	D-flat major
Taurus:	E-flat major
Gemini:	F-sharp major
Cancer:	G-sharp major
Leo:	A-sharp major
Virgo:	C major
Libra:	D major
Scorpio:	E major
Sagittarius:	F major
Capricorn:	G major
Aquarius:	A major
Pisces:	B major

Each of the Sun signs, in astrology, is equated with a specific part of the body:

Aries: Head, ears, eyes, nose, subrenal glands

Taurus: Neck, throat, organs of speech, thyroid gland

Gemini: Lungs, arms, shoulders, nerves

Cancer: Breasts, stomach, alimentary canal

Leo: Heart, spine, back

Virgo: Intestines, nervous system

Libra: Kidneys

Scorpio: Sex organs

Sagittarius: Liver, hips, thighs

Capricorn: Knees, bones, teeth

Aquarius: Ankles, shins, circulation

Pisces: Feet

You can see, then, that when working on a particular part of the body, you can arrive at the correct keynote through astrological correlation. To use the example, from above, of working for the problem of constipation, this would be the intestinal area that is

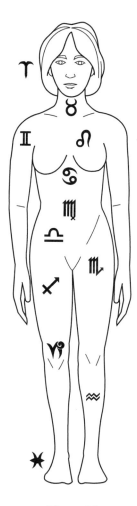

Figure 28
Body/Sun Signs Correspondences

governed by Virgo (see fig. 28). Virgo's keynote is C major. So any piece of music in the key of C major would be fitting accompaniment for the color therapy for constipation. Another example . . . working on the kidneys. Kidneys are ruled by Libra. The keynote for Libra is D major, so any piece of music in the key of D major would be good here.

As you can see, all the keynotes given are majors. It should be noted that where the problem being treated is a mentally related one, the minor key is better. The major keys have been described as "outpouring, productive, and expanding." The minor keys as "secretive, sustaining, and enfolding."

In *Healing and Regeneration Through Music* (New Age Press, Calif., 1978), Corrine Heline gives a partial list of musical *prescriptions* used by Harriet A. Seymour, of the music division of the Hospital Visiting Committee of New York:

> Of benefit to persons suffering from paralysis and disorders of the joints: Sousa's marches, *The Anvil Chorus, William Tell Overture,* Brahms' *Hungarian Dances, By the Waters of the Minnetonka.*
>
> Of benefit to persons afflicted with tuberculosis: Strauss' waltzes, *La Paloma, Minuet in G,* Schubert's *Serenade, March of the Wooden Soldiers,* Brahms' *Lullaby,* Schubert's *Ave Maria, From the Land of the Sky Blue Water, Somewhere Over the Rainbow.*

Beneficial to persons being otherwise treated for heart trouble: The *Barcarolle*, *The Blue Danube*, Chopin's *A Minor Waltz*, tango music, *Humoresque*, Cui's *Orientale*, *Song of India*, *Donna é Mobile*, Oley Speake's *Sylvia*.

For persons suffering from insomnia and from pain generally: Mendelssohn's *Spring Song*, *Meditation from Thais*, Chopin's *Preludes*, *On Wings of Song*, *Andante*, Beethoven's *Fifth Symphony*, *Adagio*, Beethoven's *Pathetique Symphony*.

For soothing persons suffering from certain mental and nervous afflictions: Rhythmic folk songs, *County Derry*, songs of Stephen Foster, Spanish tangoes, Brahm's *Hungarian Dances*, Sousa's marches, Strauss' Waltzes, Gilbert and Sullivan, *Indian Love Call*, *My Wild Irish Rose*, *Wishing*, *Estrellita*.

Radiesthesia for Diagnosis and Prescription

Radiesthesia is a science related to dowsing or divining. We have discussed the fact that all matter vibrates, radiating energy. Ellie Howe says (*Man, Myth, and Magic*, v. 17, Marshall Cavendish, N. Y., 1970):

Consider two concepts: first, that all matter radiates on its own wavelength; and second, that living organisms, meaning human beings, animals and even plants, emit electromagnetic wave radiations that depend for their intensity and frequency upon general vitality and metabolism, and in the case of human beings, and perhaps even animals, on psycho-physical tone. Thus given the identification of a 'wavelength' that appears on the basis of past experience to reflect some kind of pathological or psychical imbalance, the radiesthetic practitioner will attempt to correct the imbalance.

The pendulum is the instrument of the radiesthetic. In chapter 2, I introduced you to its use in psychic development. The electrical field that emanates from the body has both a positive and a negative charge. When a pendulum is held over the positive (usually on the right side of the body), it swings in a clockwise direction. When held over the negative (left side), it swings in a counterclockwise direction. The size of the circle in which it swings is indicative of the strength of the field. The pendulum is actually one of the most sensitive of all divining instruments and is especially suited to precise work such as medical diagnosis and treatment. This is especially recognized in Europe where medical radiesthesia is burgeoning.

Diagnosis

In radiesthetic and radionic practice there are ten general disease conditions considered. These are:

1. Virus

2. Bacterium

3. Poison

4. Allergy

5. Toxins

6. Secretion imbalance

7. Hormone imbalance

8. Mineral imbalance

9. Vitamin imbalance

10. Psychological condition

Make up a 3″ x 5″ card with these ten conditions on it, in the form of a semicircle (fig. 29).

To diagnose yourself, simply sit and concentrate on yourself, asking yourself what the condition is. Then hold the pendulum over the card and, as you keep asking, you will see it start to swing strongly to one of the ten listed conditions. If you are diagnosing someone else, hold their right hand (left, if left-handed) in your free hand and ask the pendulum about their condition. If the person you wish to enquire about cannot be present, you can get the result by simply holding something belonging to them—a

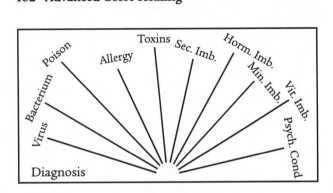

Figure 29
Condition Card for Radiesthesia

bloodspot on a piece of paper; a saliva sample in a phial; an item of personal clothing, a used handkerchief; even a good photograph (of the person alone).

To be more specific in your diagnosing, you can make up additional cards, each for one of the ten main groups, but with the particular condition broken into specifics (i.e., a list of viruses; a list of allergies; etc.). The pendulum you use for diagnosis, and for treatment (see below), should be one with a long, thin point to it, for accuracy.

Treatment

Another card will display the seven main colors, either by color or by word (fig. 30).

The swing of the pendulum will indicate the needed color to treat the ailment. Watch the pendulum carefully here. It may swing between two of the main colors, indicating an intermediate shade. Here again you could have secondary cards, one for each of the main colors, but shading gradually through to the next color on either side of it.

Another possibility is that the pendulum will swing first on one color and then on a second. This would be an indication of the need for both of those colors in the treatment.

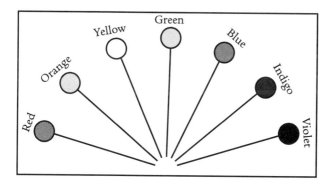

Figure 30
Treatment Card for Radiesthesia

I would recommend one more card, for daily treatment. This is especially useful if you find that more than one color is needed, since it will give the times for each—one color may be needed for the majority of the treatment time with the second color as a minor supplement (fig. 31).

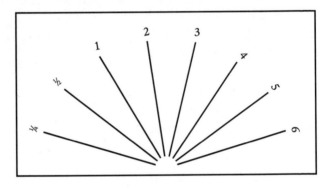

Figure 31
Duration Card for Radiesthesia

8

Color in Everyday Living

How drab our lives would be without color. Contrast looking out of your window on a dull, rainy, misty morning in the fall or winter with looking out on a bright, sunny morning in the spring or summer. The one makes you want to withdraw and seek inner warmth and brightness; the other gives you a feeling of expansion, of well-being, and positiveness. The colors in nature are so noticeable: the bright greens of grass and darker greens of leaves, the brilliant yellows of dandelions and buttercups, the bright blue of the sky

. . . in our homes we use color to brighten our lives. We paint and paper the walls of our rooms, carefully choosing curtains, drapes, and upholstery, and frequently adding a vase of flowers for "a splash of color." Color is important, psychologically and physiologically. In the booklet *Color Dynamics for the Home,* the Pittsburgh Plate Glass Company says:

> . . . results (of the use of color in industry, educational institutions, office buildings, and homes) are due to the energy in color. Color, in the form of light, is part of the electro-magnetic spectrum. . . . Variations in the number of impacts upon the eye affects muscular, mental, and nervous activity. For example, tests show that under ordinary light muscular activity is twenty-three empirical units. It advances slightly under blue light. Green light increases it a little more. Yellow light raises it to thirty units. Subject a person to a given color for as little as five minutes and his mental as well as his muscular activity changes.

It is obvious, then, that the color of your environment can have a profound effect on you and, therefore, it bears careful evaluation. In factories it has been found that absenteeism has decreased and morale, safety, even comfort, have been greatly increased by the judicious use of suitable colors.

The expert in the field of colors for home, office, school, and factory is Faber Birren, who makes his living by prescribing color. "He prescribes it to government, to education, to the armed forces, to architecture, to industry and commerce" according to his book *Color Psychology and Color Therapy* (University Books, N. Y., 1961). One of the points he deals with is *visibility*.

> Visibility is one factor in color that may be readily measured. The ability to see clearly may be determined by experiment and test and requires neither feeling nor judgment. . . . The eye sees best in white, yellowish, or yellowish-green light, and worst in blue light. Thus sunglasses are best when tinted either yellow or yellow-green. These colors may not only increase visibility and acuity by cutting down the excess brilliance of full sunlight, but they will screen out the disturbing influence of ultraviolet. In fact, on a sunny day yellow glasses may actually improve vision and help the eye to see more clearly into distance.

When speaking of environmental decoration he goes on to say:

> It is quite possible to set forth ideal brightness specifications. . . . Ceilings—almost without exception should be white. This will be essential to the efficiency of indirect lighting systems. In direct systems, the white overhead will reduce contrasts between fixtures and their surroundings. Being 'neutral,' white will also attract less psychological notice and hence prove nondistracting . . .

For industrial purposes, soft, delicately grayish hues are best. They are lacking in aggression, less distracting, and they most effectively conceal dust and soiling. Ordinarily, primitive colors such as blue and yellow are tiresome. Where subtlety exists, (blueish-green, peach, etc.) a more comfortable environment will be found and one that will "wear well" over prolonged periods. It is logical to use "cool" colors such as green or blue where the working conditions expose the employee to relatively high temperatures. Conversely, "warm" tones of ivory, cream, or peach are suitable to soften up a vaulty or chilly space and compensate for lack of natural light.

The colors we use in our personal appearance are as
important as those in our surroundings. It is here,
and in the home, that we can draw on chromology
to boost our lives. In chapter 3 I showed how,
through numerology, you can find the color(s) you
are lacking. This can be expanded to show what
color(s) you might need on a particular day, for it is
not only Mondays that can be *blue*. Many times we
feel down on other days; days when there seems no
special reason to feel that way. So let us examine days
of the week.

Some books on color give a list showing the colors generally associated with each particular day of
the week. I find these listings are not very accurate,
for not all Mondays are the same, nor all Tuesdays—
each day is individual. To find the color associated
with a particular day, then, you must return to numerology. Let us consider Friday, September 23,
1983, as an example:

$$9.23.1983 = 9 + 2 + 3 + 1 + 9 + 8 + 3 = 3 = 8$$

This particular Friday is an 8 day and, from
chapter 3, we know that 8 is associated with the
color rose.

The following Friday is September 30.

$$9.30.1983 = 33 = 6$$

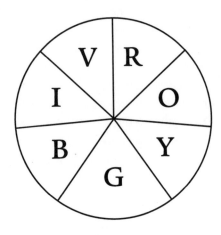

Figure 32
Opposite Colors

So that is a 6 day, or indigo. You can see, then, that not all Fridays (or any other days of the week) are the same. Now how can you use this knowledge?

If the day's color is a *positive* one, a bright, warm, uplifting one, then you probably will not want to alter it . . . just enjoy it. But supposing it is at the other end of the spectrum? Suppose, for example, that you see that this coming Tuesday is going to be a blue day and Friday a violet day? Fine—then you can be prepared for them and can counter any adverse/depressive effects by dressing accordingly. Dress in the opposite color, to counterbalance.

Opposite blue are red and orange. On Tuesday use these colors liberally. Opposite violet are yellow and green; use these colors liberally on Friday. You will find that the simple act of compensating for the less invigorating colors will keep you from getting depressed (see figure 32 for opposite colors).

Conversely, of course, you may want to ward off an overabundance of energy. On a red day, you may prefer to wear blue and green, or turquoise, and take it easy.

Color Treasure Maps

There is a magickal technique used to help in creating your own reality. It is the Treasure Map. Through the Treasure Map it is possible to manifest virtually anything that you desire. As a road map shows you how to get to your destination, so a Treasure Map helps you achieve your goals. It can be large or small; with or without elaborate pictures. Whatever its composition, it is a means of keeping your intent on your goal; of keeping you always moving forward toward what you desire.

The very act of making a Treasure Map is a ritual for success. When making a magickal talisman (see chapter 5), you put *power,* or mana, into it by working on it personally; by directing your energies into it. So with the Treasure Map. And by incorporating color in its construction, you can really create an abundance of power, as you will see.

Many people feel that they are *not worthy* of the good things in life. Or, perhaps through ingrained Christian or other religious training, feel that it is somehow *wrong* to have material possessions and/or wealth. Nothing could be further from the truth. We are all worthy of, and fully entitled to, the Universal Abundance. It is as much *right* for you to have what you want, as it is for anyone else to. The more you keep that thought in mind, the sooner you will achieve your desires. And the Treasure Map will make it happen.

It may seem unbelievable that simply by drawing and coloring pictures you can get what you want. It seems especially so when you can not draw too well and your efforts look like those of a nine-year-old child! But do not despair . . . nine-year-olds generally have a lot of psychic energy.

Your map should be as simple as possible, with clear, vivid pictures (we will consider the pictureless one later). At the top center you need a picture of the *source* of all things. This could be a God- or Goddess-like figure, or a symbol (such as the infinity sign, the Chinese yin-yang, a pentagram, cross, or star of David), or what to you personally is indicative of the *Source*.

Now show (draw) what you want, coming from this Source to you. Suppose, for example, you want

Figure 33
Treasure Map

enough money to buy a car. Then you might draw a Treasure Map something like that shown in figure 33.

As you see, everything comes from the Source to you. I find it good to work in three steps—(1) (on the left of the Treasure Map) acknowledgement that everything comes from the Source; (2) (center) affirming that I have what I want, and that I have it now; (3) (right of the Treasure Map) giving thanks for receiving what I wanted.

The standard of drawing is not important. In fact I would go so far as to say that the more basic it is, the better, almost make it a caricature. In other words, do not try for photographic realism. And—most importantly—use lots of bright colors. If you are a blonde, for example, draw yourself with bright yellow hair. Let the Source—be it God, Goddess, Jesus, ankh, pentagram, or what/whomever—be surrounded with all the colors.

Some people suggest that you find appropriate pictures in magazines and cut them out, pasting them on to make your Treasure Map. I think you will find it much more effective to do all the illustrating yourself. This way, there are far more of your energies going into the map, plus it is exactly what you want, and not a compromise of any sort.

A pictureless Treasure Map can be made, if you really feel that you can not draw at all; instead of the pictures, then, you simply write out, in plain, simple terms, exactly what it is you want. Use as few words as possible and, again, use bright colors for writing them. But, I would again emphasize that artistic skills are not important. It will be far better to draw—however simply; however crudely—than to spell it out.

What do you do with the map after it is made? Hang it somewhere where you will see it frequently. Tape it to the refrigerator door, to the side of a filing cabinet, to your bedroom wall. Put it somewhere where you can keep looking at it and keep going over, in your mind, all that it shows. Get to where you can see it in your mind's eye when you are riding the bus or train to work, when you are jogging, when you are sleeping. Constantly seeing, and repeating, what the Treasure Map shows will take you to your destination. It will not happen overnight, but it will happen.

Treasure Maps can be done for possessions, for jobs, love, health, business success, spiritual advancement . . . for anything. They are fun to do, but, most importantly, they work. Remember—basic drawings and bright colors.

You can incorporate some of what you have learned about color correspondences when making your map. For instance, if you are working for money, draw your map on green paper. Working for love? Use pink paper. Tranquility? Blue paper, and so on.

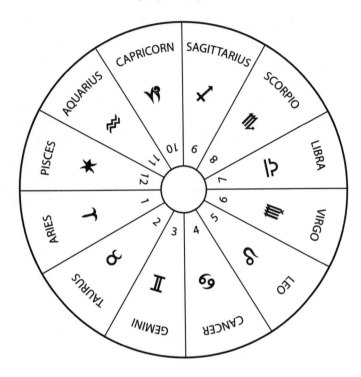

Figure 34
Astrological Chart

Suppose you want a number of things at one time? Well, there is no reason why you should not put them all on one Treasure Map. A good idea, here, is to pattern it after the wheel of astrology. The astrological chart is divided up into twelve sections, known as houses. These are equated with the signs of the zodiac—the First House is Aries, the

Second House is Taurus, and so on (fig. 34). Additionally, each house is equated with a particular area of life:

First House: Temperament; outward behavior; appearance; health.

Second House: Possessions; financial condition.

Third House: Brothers; sisters; communication; perceptive abilities; studies; mental aptitudes.

Fourth House: One of the parents; real estate; the home; domestic affairs; the beginning and the end of life.

Fifth House: Speculation; love affairs; pets; sexual urges; creative expressions.

Sixth House: Servants; sickness; hygiene; relationships between employer and employee; veterinarians.

Seventh House: Marriage partners; business partners; open (obvious) enemies; contracts.

Eighth House: Partner's money; attitude toward life and death; gifts; surgery.

Ninth House: Religious and philosophical outlooks; long journeys; foreigners and foreign countries; publishing; psychic development.

Tenth House: Standing in the community; reputation; social status; employment; the other parent (from the one in the Fourth House).

Eleventh House: Friends; social alliances; financial condition of employer; income from business when self-employed.

Twelfth House: Secret enemies; large animals; clandestine affairs; hospitalization; isolation; service to others.

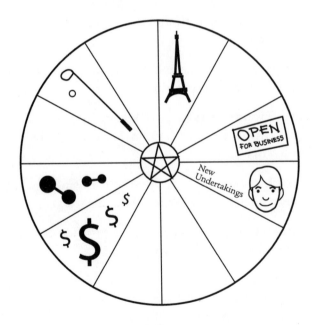

Figure 35
Treasure Map Based on Astrology

Suppose you want to improve your financial situation, take a trip to Europe, go into partnership to start a business with a friend, join the local country club, and do some body building?

Financial situation would be covered in the Second House. Long journeys are in the Ninth. Partnerships are in the Seventh, and do not forget that the Fifth House also covers new undertakings. The Eleventh deals with social alliances, which would cover your country club aspirations. And the First House deals with your outward appearance. You could, then, do a Treasure Map, something like that shown in Figure 35.

In addition to using bright colors in the whole rendition, consider also the colors associated with the astrological Sun signs and, through them, with each of the houses: Aries, red; Taurus, yellow; Gemini, violet; Cancer, green; Leo, orange; Virgo, violet; Libra, yellow; Scorpio, red; Sagittarius, purple; Capricorn, blue; Aquarius, indigo; Pisces, indigo. You could use those colors to do the backgrounds of those houses you are using.

Afterword

*I*f nothing else, I hope that this book has sparked your interest in color and its many uses. As I said in the Introduction, "Since the beginning of time, colors have been endowed with magick." I have here shown a few simple ways to use that magick, for better health, wealth, and happiness. It is a form of magick that anyone can use, without elaborate equipment, without special training, and especially without any danger. It is practical.

Do the color meditations. Try the divination. Experiment with the magick. Make

Treasure Maps and do healing. And try your own experiments and variations. The beneficial uses of magick are almost infinite. I have included what I believe to be one of the most comprehensive bibliographies available on the subject. Use it. Read every book you can and open for yourself the *rainbow of existence* . . . a life filled with color.

Raymond Buckland

Bibliography

Abbott, Arthur G. *The Mysteries of Color.* Chicago, Ill.: Aries Press, 1977.

Amber, Reuben B. *Color Therapy.* New York, N.Y.: Aurora Press, 1983.

Anderson, Mary. *Color Healing.* York Beach, Maine: Samuel Weiser, 1975.

Andrews, Ted. *How to Heal with Color.* St. Paul, Minn.: Llewellyn Publications, 1992.

Babbitt, Edwin D. *The Principles of Light and Color*. New York, N.Y.: Babbitt, 1878.

Basford, L and J. Pick. *The Rays of Light*. London, 1966.

Bhattacharyya, B. *Vibgyor, The Science of Cosmic Ray Therapy*. Baroda, India: Good Companions, 1957.

Birren, Faber. *Color Psychology and Color Therapy*. New York, N.Y.: University Books, 1961.

——. *New Horizons in Color*. New York, N.Y.: Reinhold, 1955.

Boos-Hamburger, H. *The Creative Power of Color*. Sussex, England: New Knowledge Books (n.d.).

Bragg, William, *The Universe of Light*. New York, N.Y.: Dover, 1959.

Brunler, Oscar. *Rays and Radiation Phenomona*. DeVorss, Calif.: 1948.

Butler, W.E. *How to Read the Aura*. New York, N.Y.: Samuel Weiser, 1971.

Cayce, Edgar. *Gems and Stones*. Virginia Beach, Va.: A.R.E. Press, 1976.

——. *Auras*. Virginia Beach, Va.: A.R.E. Press, 1973.

Chevreul, M. E. *The Principles of Harmony and Contrast of Colors.* London: Bell & Dalby, 1870.

Chrapowicki, Maryla de. *The Power of Sound and Health, Strength and Union.* London: Medical Society for the Study of Radiesthesia (n.d.).

———. *SpectroBiology.* Mokilumne Hill, Calif.: Health Research, 1938.

Clark, Linda. *The Ancient Art of Color Therapy.* Old Greenwich, Conn.: Devin-Adair, 1975.

Clark, L., and V. Martine. *Health, Youth and Beauty Through Color Breathing.* Millbrae, Calif.: Celestial Arts, 1976.

Clement, Mark. *Waves that Heal.* Calif.: Health Research (n.d.)

Cooper-Hunt, C. L. *Radiesthetic Analysis.* Mokilumne Hill, Calif.: Health Research, 1969.

Copen, Bruce. *Heal Yourself with Color.* Sussex, England: Academic Publications, 1974.

———. *Character Analysis with Color.* Sussex, England: Academic Publications, 1976.

Corte, L. P. *Sound and Vibration Measurement.* London: Medical Society for the Study of Radiesthesia (n.d.).

Don, Frank. *Color Your World*. New York, N.Y.: Warner Destiny Books, 1977.

Evans, Ralph, M. *An Introduction to Color*. New York, N.Y.: Wiley, 1948.

Fernie, W. T. *Precious Stones (Curative)*. Bristol, England: Wright, 1907.

Fielding, William, J. *The Marvels and Oddities of Sunlight*. Girard, Kans.: Haldeman-Julius (n.d.)

Finch, W. J. & E. *Photo-Chromotherapy*. Az.: Esoteric Publications, 1972.

Ghadiali, Dinshah P. *Spectro-Chrome Metry Encyclopaedia*. Vols. 1, 2, 3. Malaga, N.J.: Spectro-Chrome Institute, 1939.

———. *Family Health Protector*. Malaga, N.J.: Spectro-Chrome Institute, 1943.

Goethe, Johann W. von. *Theory of Colours*. London: John Murray, 1840

Graves, Maitland. *The Art of Color and Design*. New York, N.Y.: McGraw-Hill, 1941.

———. *Color Fundamentals*. New York, N.Y.: McGraw-Hill, 1952.

Hanoka, N. S. *The Advantages of Healing by Visible Spectrum Therapy.* Ghaziabad, India: Bharti Association, 1957.

Hebing, J. *Letters on the Theory of Colour.* Sussex, England: New Knowledge Books (n.d.).

Heline, Corinne. *Healing and Regeneration through Color.* Calif.: New Age Press, 1976.

——. *Healing and Regeneration through Music.* La Canada, Calif.: New Age Press, 1978.

Hetherington, Rex D. *Color—Its Power, Action and Therapeutic Value.* Boston, Ma. (n.p., n.d.).

Hoffman, Enid. *Huna, A Beginner's Guide.* Gloucester, Mass.: Para Research, 1976.

Howat, R. D. *Elements of Chromotherapy.* London: Actinic, 1938.

Hunt, Roland T. *Complete Color Prescription.* Los Angeles, Calif.: Devorss, 1962.

——. *The Seven Keys to Color Healing.* London: C. W. Daniel, 1971.

——. *The Eighth Key to Color.* London: Fowler, 1965.

——. *Fragrant and Radiant Healing Symphony.* London: (n.p.), 1937.

Jackson, Carole. *Color Me Beautiful.* New York, N.Y.: Ballantine Books, 1980.

Jacobson, Egbert. *Basic Colour.* Theobald, Ill.: (n.p.), 1948.

Jensen, Dr. E. T. *Some Steps in Radiesthetic Technique.* London, England: Medical Society for the Study of Radiesthesia (n.d.).

Kargere, Audrey. *Color and Personality.* New York, N.Y.: Wehman (n.d.).

Katz, David. *The World of Color.* London: Kegan Paul, 1935.

Kelly, K. L., and D. B. Judd. *Color—Universal Language and Dictionary of Names.* Washington, D.C., U.S. Dept. of Commerce, 1976.

Kilner, Walter J. *The Aura.* New York, N.Y.: Samuel Weiser, 1973.

Klein, Adrian B. *Colour-Music.* London: Lockwood, 1930.

Ladd-Franklin, Christine. *Colour and Colour Theories.* New York, N.Y.: Von Nostrand, 1929.

Leadbetter, C. W. *Man Visible and Invisible.* London: Theosophical Society, 1971.

Lewis, Roger. *Color and the Edgar Cayce Readings.* Va.: A.R.E. Press, 1973.

Luckiesh, Matthew. *Color and Its Implications.* New York, N.Y.: Van Nostrand, 1921.

———. *Ultra Violet Radiation.* New York, N.Y.: Van Nostrand, 1922.

———. *Color and Colors.* New York, N.Y.: Van Nostrand, 1938.

Luckeish, M. and A. J. Pacini. *Light and Health.* Baltimore, Md.: Williams & Williams, 1926.

Maerz, A. & M. P. Paul. *A Dictionary of Color.* New York, N.Y.: McGraw-Hill, 1930.

Mayer, Gladys. *Colour and Healing.* Sussex, England: New Knowledge Books, 1974.

———. *The Mystery—Wisdom of Colour.* Sussex, England: New Knowledge Books (n.d.).

———. *Colour and the Human Soul.* Sussex, England: New Knowledge Books (n.d.).

Mermet, Abbé. *Principles and Practices of Radiesthesia.* London: Watkins, 1975.

Ostwald, Wilhelm. *Colour Science.* London: Winsor & Newton, 1931.

Ott, John N. *Health and Light*. New York, N.Y.: Pocket Books, 1976.

Ouseley, S. G. J. *Color Meditations*. Essex, England: Fowler, 1949.

——. *The Power of the Rays*. Essex, England: Fowler, 1951.

PanCoast, S. *Blue and Red Light*. Philadelphia, Pa.: Stoddart, 1877.

Pittsburgh Plate Glass Company. *Color Dynamics for the Home*. Tallahassee, Fla.: P. P. G. Co. (n.d.).

Ramadahn. *Colour and Healing for the New Age*. London: Roberts (n.d.).

Richards, Dr. Guyon. *Medical Dowsing*. London: Medical Society for the Study of Radiesthesia (n.d.).

Sandback, John. *The Mysteries of Color*. Chicago, Ill.: Aries Press, 1977.

Sander, C. G. *Colour in Health and Disease*. London: Daniel, 1926.

——. *The Seven Keys of Colour Healing*. London: Daniel, 1928.

Sargent, Walter. *The Enjoyment and Use of Color*. New York, N.Y.: Scribners, 1923.

Scott, Ian (tr. & ed.) *The Lüscher Color Test of Dr. Max Lüscher.* New York, N.Y.: Random House, 1969.

Steiner, Rudolf. *Colour.* Sussex, England: New Knowledge Books (n.d.).

Stevens, Ernest J. *Lights, Colors, Tones, and Nature's Finer Forces.* San Francisco, Calif.: Stevens, 1923.

Sturzaker, D. & J. *Colour and the Kabbalah.* New York, N.Y.: Samuel Weiser, 1975.

Tarpey, Kingsley. *Healing by Radiesthesia.* London, England: Medical Society for the Study of Radiesthesia (n.d.).

Thedick, Eleanore. *The Bridge of Color.* Sacramento, Calif.: Christ Ministry Foundation (n.d.).

Thronton, Dr. R. G. *Rays, Radiations, and the Psychophysical Organism.* London, England: Medical Society for the Study of Radiesthesia (n.d.).

Time-Life Books. *Color.* New York, N.Y.: 1970.

Tom Linson, Dr. H. *The Use of the Pendulum in Medicine.* London, England: Medical Society for the Study of Radiesthesia (n.d.).

Turner, Albert E. *A Study of Color.* Pts. I, II, III, The Searchlight, v. 15 no. 8 (Aug. 1963), v. 15 no. 11 (Nov. 1963), v. 16 no. 2 (Feb. 1964) Virginia, Va.: A.R.E. Press (n.d.).

Verhoven, Marion. "Music Therapy," *Chinese Magazine* (Spring 1952).

Wethered, Vernon D. *The Practice of Medical Radiesthesia.* London: C. W. Daniel, 1977.

Willey, Raymond C. *Modern Dowsing.* Phoenix, Az.: Esoteric Publications, 1976.

Wilson, M. *What is Color?* Sussex, England: New Knowledge Books (n.d.).

Wright, W. D. *The Measurement of Colour.* London: Hilger, 1944.

Journals

Radionic Quarterly Journal of the Radionic Association, Guildford, Surrey, England.

Radiesthesia Journal of the Medical Society for the Study of Radiesthesia, London, England.

Index

REACH FOR THE MOON

Llewellyn publishes hundreds of books on your favorite subjects! To get these exciting books, including the ones on the following pages, check your local bookstore or order them directly from Llewellyn.

Order by Phone
- Call toll-free within the U.S. and Canada, 1-877-NEW-WRLD
- In Minnesota, call (651) 291-1970
- We accept VISA, MasterCard, and American Express

Order by Mail
- Send the full price of your order (MN residents add 7% sales tax) in U.S. funds, plus postage & handling to:

  Llewellyn Worldwide
  P.O. Box 64383, Dept. 0-7387-0204-8
  St. Paul, MN 55164–0383, U.S.A.

Postage & Handling
- **Standard** (U.S., Mexico, & Canada)

If your order is:

    $20 or under, add $5

    $20.01–$100, add $6

    Over $100, shipping is free

(Continental U.S. orders ship UPS. AK, HI, PR, & P.O. Boxes ship USPS 1st class. Mex. & Can. ship PMB.)

- **Second Day Air** (Continental U.S. only): $10 for one book plus $1 per each additional book
- **Express** (AK, HI, & PR only) [Not available for P.O. Box delivery. For street address delivery only.]: $15 for one book plus $1 per each additional book
- **International Surface Mail:** $20 or under, add $5 plus $1 per item; $20.01 and over, add $6 plus $1 per item
- **International Airmail:** Books—Add the retail price of each item; Non-book items—Add $5 per item

> **Please allow 4–6 weeks for delivery on all orders.**
> **Postage and handling rates subject to change.**

Discounts
We offer a 20% discount to group leaders or agents. You must order a minimum of 5 copies of the same book to get our special quantity price.

Free Catalog
Get a free copy of our color catalog, *New Worlds of Mind and Spirit*. Subscribe for just $10.00 in the United States and Canada ($30.00 overseas, airmail). Call 1-877-NEW-WRLD today!

Visit our website at www.llewellyn.com for more information.

Practical Candleburning Rituals

Spells & Rituals for Every Purpose

RAYMOND BUCKLAND, PH.D.

Magick is a way in which to apply the full range of your hidden psychic powers to the problems we all face in daily life. We know that normally we use only 5 percent of our total powers. Magick taps powers from deep inside our psyche where we are in contact with the universe's limitless resources.

Magick need not be complex—it can be as simple as using a few candles to focus your mind, a simple ritual to give direction to your desire, a few words to give expression to your wish.

This book shows you how easy it can be. Here is magick for fun; magick as a craft; magick for success, love, luck, money, marriage, and healing. Practice magick to stop slander, to learn truth, to heal an unhappy marriage, to overcome a bad habit, to break up a love affair, etc.

0-87542-048-6
208 pp., 5¼ x 8, illus. $7.95

Also available in Spanish.